feminist
measures in
survey research

feminist measures in survey research

Catherine E. Harnois
Wake Forest University

Los Angeles | London | New Delhi
Singapore | Washington DC

Los Angeles | London | New Delhi
Singapore | Washington DC

FOR INFORMATION:

SAGE Publications, Inc.
2455 Teller Road
Thousand Oaks, California 91320
E-mail: order@sagepub.com

SAGE Publications Ltd.
1 Oliver's Yard
55 City Road
London, EC1Y 1SP
United Kingdom

SAGE Publications India Pvt. Ltd.
B 1/l 1 Mohan Cooperative Industrial Area
Mathura Road, New Delhi 110 044
India

SAGE Publications Asia-Pacific Pte. Ltd.
33 Pekin Street #02-01
Far East Square
Singapore 048763

Acquisitions Editor: Vicki Knight
Associate Editor: Lauren Habib
Editorial Assistant: Kalie Koscielak
Production Editor: Brittany Bauhaus
Copy Editor: Patricia Sutton
Typesetter: Hurix Systems Pvt. Ltd.
Proofreader: Caryne Brown
Indexer: Terri Corry
Cover Designer: Anupama Krishnan
Marketing Manager: Helen Salmon
Permissions Editor: Adele Hutchinson

Copyright © 2013 by SAGE Publications, Inc.

Printed in the United States of America

Library of Congress Cataloging-in-Publication Data

Harnois, Catherine E.
Feminist measures in survey research/Catherine E. Harnois.

p. cm.
Includes bibliographical references and index.

ISBN 978-1-4129-8835-3 (pbk.)

1. Feminism–Research–Methodology. 2. Social sciences–Research–Methodology. 3. Feminist theory. 4. Social surveys. I. Title.

HQ1180.H366 2013

305.4201--dc23

2011039059

This book is printed on acid-free paper.

Certified Chain of Custody
Promoting Sustainable Forestry
www.sfiprogram.org
SFI-01268

SUSTAINABLE FORESTRY INITIATIVE

SFI label applies to text stock

11 12 13 14 15 10 9 8 7 6 5 4 3 2 1

Brief Contents

Detailed Contents

About the Author

Catherine E. Harnois is an assistant professor in the Department of Sociology at Wake Forest University, where she teaches courses on social inequality and research methods. Her research focuses on multiracial feminist theories and inequalities of race, class, and gender. Some of her recent publications include "Gendered Measures, Gendered Models: Toward an Intersectional Analysis of Racial Discrimination" (with Mosi Ifatunji, 2011) and "Re-presenting Feminism: Past, Present & Future" (2008). She lives in Winston-Salem, North Carolina, with her partner, Joe, and their dog, Gussie.

Acknowledgments

Researching and writing this book has taken several years, and would not have been possible without a supportive network of colleagues, friends, and family. I first began thinking about feminist research methods while a graduate student in the sociology department at the University of North Carolina (UNC) at Chapel Hill. Andrew Perrin, Judith Blau, Barbara Risman, Karolyn Tyson, and Susan Bickford all served on my dissertation committee and provided tremendous support for my interdisciplinary exploration of contemporary feminism. Rachel Rosenfeld was also a valuable mentor for me at UNC, and she remains a source of inspiration.

At Wake Forest University, I have been fortunate to have a number of generous colleagues who have helped me to see this project from start to finish. In particular, I am grateful to Ian Taplin, Saylor Breckenridge, and Robin Simon, each of whom read excerpts of the book and gave me much-needed critical feedback. For the past two years I have participated in an interdisciplinary feminist reading and writing group funded by the Wake Forest University Humanities Institute. The members of this group, Sally Barbour, Mary DeShazer, Alessandra Beasley Von Burg, and Sandya Hewamanne, each read sections of the book and provided me with valuable feedback and encouragement. Collectively, they have taught me much about feminist theory within the humanities, and have strengthened my belief in the potential for interdisciplinary feminist scholarship.

In addition to these individuals, I am grateful for the support given to me by Wake Forest University (WFU). The WFU Office of Research and Sponsored Programs provided me with financial support at the early stages of this project, as did the Newcomb College Center for Research on Women at Tulane University. Amanda Lucas and Brooke Gilmore both worked with me as undergraduate research fellows through the Wake Forest University undergraduate research fellowship program. Brooke and Amanda helped me to assess the current state of feminist survey research, and to think more clearly about how it might be transformed by a multiracial feminist perspective.

Vicki Knight at Sage Publications has guided me through the publication process, and it has been a wonderful experience to work with and learn from her. She has been a strong source of support and encouragement from the proposal stages onward, and her feedback has undoubtedly strengthened the book. I am also grateful to the individual reviewers who took the time to carefully read and evaluate the book proposal and manuscript. In particular, I would like to thank Emily W. Kane at Bates College, Alyssa N. Zucker at the George Washington University, Jo Reger at Oakland University, Cynthia Deitch at the George Washington University, Jana L. Jasinski at the University of Central Florida, Gwen Moore at the University at Albany, Stephanie Riger at the University of Illinois at Chicago, Cynthia Deitch at the George Washington University, Patricia L. Wasielewski at the University of Redlands, Lori E. Koelsch at Duquesne University, R. Todd Coy at Colby-Sawyer College, Stella Oh at Loyola Marymount University, Natalie J. Bourdon at Mercer University, Yasemin Besen-Cassino at Montclair State University, Celeste Montoya at the University of Colorado, Boulder, and Diana O'Brien at Washington University, St. Louis.

In this and other projects, I am deeply indebted to Michele Tracy Berger and Tanya Golash-Boza for their outstanding mentoring and endless encouragement. I also want to formally acknowledge the support given to me by my life partner, Joe Harrington, without whom this book would not have been possible.

Preface

This book aims to make feminist theory, and multiracial feminist theory in particular, more accessible and relevant to survey researchers. I ask, How can multiracial feminism inform social science survey research? What would it mean, in practical terms, to bring an "intersectional" approach to survey design and statistical analysis? and How might such an approach change our conclusions about the social world?

My argument, in brief, is that multiracial feminist theorizing has tremendous untapped potential for transforming—and improving—survey research in the social sciences. To begin with, multiracial feminist scholarship offers substantive insights into the social world that have been underused by survey researchers. In addition, multiracial feminist theorizing offers survey researchers a number of specific analytic interventions that can bring greater complexity and nuance to social science research. And finally, by highlighting difference, inequality, relationality, and the context of discovery, a multiracial feminist perspective can help survey researchers to increase the quality of social science research.

It is not that multiracial feminism requires some new statistical test or advanced modeling procedure. Rather, as I hope to show in the following chapters, a multiracial feminist approach enables a critical reexamination of the basic assumptions embedded in our everyday research practices. Ultimately, I believe that multiracial feminist theory provides a new and important framework for critiquing and producing survey research on a wide range of issues.

In the chapters that follow, I focus on issues of sexism, racism, and feminism to demonstrate the potential of a multiracial feminist approach. In Chapter 2, I investigate how scholars in sociology, political science, psychology, and women's studies have used survey research to understand contemporary feminism. I find that researchers in each of these fields tend to approach survey research in different ways and that each disciplinary approach is well suited to capturing some, but not other, aspects of multiracial feminism. As such, I argue that a comprehensive multiracial feminist approach requires scholars to move beyond narrow disciplinary boundaries, to engage with the theoretical and methodological insights from a variety of intellectual fields, and to situate their own research within a broader intellectual context.

In Chapters 3, 4, and 5, I demonstrate several different approaches for bringing a multiracial feminist framework to social science survey research. Chapter 3 shows how a multiracial feminist approach can inform research using large-scale general surveys; Chapter 4 shows how such an approach might inform surveys that use multi-item scales. In Chapter 5, I show how a multiracial feminist approach can inform small-scale survey research rooted in the particular. Substantively, Chapter 3 focuses on sexism, Chapter 4 on racism, and Chapter 5 on feminism. Within each chapter, I highlight issues of meaning, measurement, and modeling, and show how multiracial feminist theorizing can inform each aspect of survey research. While each chapter can be read as a stand-alone case study, it is my hope that they are read together as a whole. Taken together, they illustrate that there are multiple ways to do multiracial feminist survey research, and this multiplicity is itself an integral part of a multiracial feminist approach.

In my concluding chapter, I bring together the methodological findings from the previous chapters and outline six considerations for thinking about survey research from a multiracial feminist perspective. Multiracial feminist survey research can take a variety of different forms, only a few of which are outlined in this text. My hope is that the considerations I outline in Chapter 6 stimulate the minds and imaginations of researchers interested in developing further approaches to multiracial feminist survey research.

One final note on language—many scholars use the terms *intersectional* and *intersectionality* rather than *multiracial feminist theory*. Though there is substantial overlap between intersectionality and multiracial feminist theory, throughout this book I emphasize the latter term. Following Baca Zinn and Thornton Dill (1996), I use the language of multiracial feminist theory because for me, it highlights the importance of racial minority women and feminist politics and activism in the intellectual genealogy of contemporary intersectional scholarship. In addition, I appreciate the emphasis on "theory." As intersectionality becomes more mainstream, there is considerable risk of its becoming a "buzzword" (Davis, 2008) and, in the process, the risk of losing both its theoretical complexity and radical potential. The phrase "multiracial feminist theory" reminds me that differences must be *theorized* and that the most important intellectual work in this area has been done by women of color, that is, by multiracial feminists.

Feminist Theory and Survey Research

"The idea that there is only 'one road' to the feminist revolution, and only one type of 'truly feminist' research, is as limiting and as offensive as male-biased accounts of research that have gone before."

~Liz Stanley and Sue Wise, 1983, p. 26.

Introduction

Over the past three decades, feminist methodologists have hammered home one point with surprising regularity: *Feminist research* takes a variety of legitimate forms; there is no "distinctive feminist method of research" (Harding, 1987; see also Chafetz, 2004a, 2004b; Fonow & Cook, 2005; Hawkesworth, 2006; Hesse-Biber, 2007; Risman, Sprague, & Howard, 1993; and Sprague, 2005). And yet, to this day, the relationship between feminist theory and *quantitative social science research* remains uneasy. Among feminist scholars, quantitative research is often seen as suspect for its association with *positivism* and its pretense of objectivity (among other things). At the same time, among quantitative researchers, feminist-identified work is often dismissed as "biased," "activist," or "substantively marginal." While a number of scholars have recently published works outlining a "feminist" approach to social science research, these books have generally steered clear of quantitative survey research. Some authors of feminist methods texts limit their discussion of feminist survey research to a small section (e.g., Hesse-Biber, 2007; Reinharz, 1992; Sprague, 2005), while others overlook survey research entirely (e.g., Hesse-Biber, Gilmartin, & Lydenberg, 1999; Jaggar, 2008; Naples, 2003). Sociologist Joey Sprague (2005) aptly describes the situation:

> Because feminists and other critical researchers have tended to assume that quantitative methodology cannot respond to their concerns, there are relatively few analyses of specific procedures that are problematic in mainstream quantitative methodology and there is even less written on feminist ways of implementing experiments or surveys. (pp. 81–82)

In this book, I hope to offer a new approach for viewing (and doing!) quantitative feminist research. Rather than asking, Can quantitative research *really* be feminist? (as many other feminist methodologists have already asked and answered), I ask, What do quantitative researchers risk by continuing to ignore feminist theories? My answer, which I happily reveal up front, is, A lot! Though a feminist approach will certainly add more to some branches of quantitative research than to others, a feminist perspective can inform virtually every aspect of the research process, from survey design to statistical modeling, to the theoretical frameworks used to interpret results. Throughout the book, I hope to show how feminist theory can measurably and significantly improve a wide range of quantitative social science research. In addition, I want to suggest that the relationship between quantitative research and feminist theory is especially fruitful when an interdisciplinary, multiracial feminist approach is used.

Those who are relatively unfamiliar with both feminist theory and quantitative research and those who have already discovered for themselves the usefulness of integrating feminist theory and quantitative methods may see the aforementioned goals as relatively straightforward: I hope to show how a multiracial feminist approach can improve quantitative social science research in a variety of areas. Readers with a background in the humanities, feminist philosophies of science, postmodern feminist theories, or queer theories, however, are likely to see these goals as something else: complex, perhaps even misguided or naive. As psychologist Carolyn Wood Sherif (1979/1987, p. 51) wrote some thirty years ago, "If the issues of [gender] bias in psychological research were as simple as turning the methods and instruments prized by psychology into the service of defeating bias, many battles would have been won long ago." Readers who approach this book with a background in social science are, perhaps, just as likely to view my aims as suspect. Science infused explicitly with ideology and activist agendas is no longer science, one might argue. As Janet Saltzman Chafetz (2004a), sociologist and self-described feminist, asserted,

> although there is such a thing as feminist theory—even if I do not think of it as social scientific—I find the very idea of feminist methodology in the social and behavioral sciences fundamentally untenable. . . . The research design and tools of data collection and analysis one selects ought to be chosen on the basis that they are the most appropriate to answering a given research question (pp. 971–972)

—not on the basis of political or ideological commitments.

My goal in this book, then, is to address both of these concerns head-on. I argue that feminist theory and survey research *can* be used together. In fact, much existing research already points to the advantages of feminist social science research. At the same time, however, elements of Sherif's and Chafetz's comments ring true. A feminist approach to social science research does require something other than redeploying the same old instruments and methods (recall feminist theorist Audre Lorde's similar assertion that "the master's tools will never dismantle the master's house" [1984, pp. 110–113]). And while I certainly disagree with Chafetz on the tenability of feminist methodology, I wholeheartedly agree with her second point. The research design and tools of data collection and analysis *should* be chosen on the basis that they are the most appropriate to answering a given research question. As I hope to show in this book, however, a multi-racial feminist approach is oftentimes the most appropriate choice.

In the remainder of this chapter, I provide a brief introduction to feminist theory and research. I begin with the question, What makes research "feminist"? and then examine the historically uneasy relationship between quantitative social science research and feminist research. After exploring how other scholars have navigated this relationship, I then focus on one particular branch of feminist theory—multiracial feminism—which has been largely ignored in quantitative social science research.

In considering the relationship between multiracial feminist theory and quantitative social science research, I introduce three themes that together form the backbone of this book. First, multiracial feminist theories offer numerous substantive insights into the social world that have been under-used by social science researchers. Second, multiracial feminist theorizing offers survey researchers a number of analytic interventions that can bring increased complexity and nuance to their research. And third, by highlighting difference, inequality, relationality, and the context of discovery, a multiracial feminist perspective can help survey researchers increase the quality of social science research. I describe the tenets of multiracial feminism and conclude this chapter with an overview of what is to come.

What is Feminist Research?

More than 30 years ago, historian Gerda Lerner called for a feminist transformation in the field of history. She wrote,

> [H]istory as traditionally recorded and interpreted by historians has been, in
> fact, the history of the activities of men ordered by male values—one might
> properly call it "men's History." Women have barely figured in it; the few who
> were noticed at all were members of families or relatives of important men
> and, very occasionally and exceptionally, women who performed roles gener-
> ally reserved for men. In the face of such monumental neglect, the effort to
> reconstruct a female past has been called "Women's History." The term must
> be understood not as being descriptive of a past reality, but as both a *concep-
> tual model and a strategy* by which to focus on and isolate that which tradi-
> tional history has obscured. (1979, pp. 168–169, italics added for emphasis)

In her approach to women's history, Lerner called for something more than
simply "finding women" in the historical record. She argued that the development of women's history would require "challenging traditional sources,"
challenging the "traditional periodization of history," redefining categories
and values, in short, a complete paradigm shift. "Women's history," she
writes, "demands a fundamental re-evaluation of the assumptions and methodology of traditional history and traditional thought" (1979, p. 180).

Over the course of the next decade, similar arguments were made throughout the humanities and social sciences. Sociologists Judith Stacey and Barrie
Thorne, for example, called for a feminist revolution that would "transform
the basic conceptual frameworks" of sociology (1985, p. 301). In addition to
"correcting sexist biases" in research, and "creating new topics" that reflect
women's experiences, the feminist revolution they called for would produce a
"'gendered' understanding of all aspects of human culture and relationships"
and would "as equally attend to race, class, and sexuality as to gender"
(1985, p. 311). In the same year, psychologist Michelle Fine published an
article assessing the development of feminist psychology. She concluded that
while some advances had been made, future feminist scholarship would be
strengthened by situating individuals within social and historical contexts,
increasing cross-disciplinary collaboration among researchers, and by "documenting the diversity of women's experiences" (1985, p. 179). For purposes
of this book, what is most interesting about these accounts is that these scholars see a feminist approach to scholarship as something more than "research
about women." For Lerner, Fine, Stacey and Thorne, and others, a feminist
perspective challenges some of the most taken-for-granted conceptual and
methodological assumptions in a given field.

Feminist research requires a different approach to scholarship, but what does that approach entail? The answer depends on whom one asks. For example, feminist philosopher Sandra Harding (1987, p. 1) begins her classic book, *Feminism and Methodology,* by explicitly rejecting the idea that there is a "distinctive feminist method of research." She brings a historical approach to feminist social science, asking, "What are the characteristics that distinguish the most illuminating examples of feminist research?" (p. 6). She identifies three. First, feminist research "generates its problematics from the perspective of women's experiences." Second, it is scholarship done *for* women—it seeks to provide women with explanations that they "want and need." And third, feminist research emphasizes the "importance of studying ourselves and 'studying up,' instead of 'studying down.'" In other words, feminist inquiry "locates the researcher in the same critical plane as the overt subject matter" (p. 8). In their book, *Beyond Methodology*, Mary Margaret Fonow and Judith A. Cook (1991, p. 2) identify four themes in feminist research, "reflexivity; an action orientation; attention to the affective components of the research; and use of the situation-at-hand." Feminist approaches to social research, they explain, are "often characterized by an emphasis on creativity, spontaneity, and improvisation in the selection of both topic and method" (1991, p. 11). In her *Handbook of Feminist Research*, sociologist Sharlene Hesse-Biber (2007, pp. 16–17) describes feminists' research in a similar way: It asks new questions, "going beyond correcting gender bias in dominant research studies"; centralizes issues of power, authority, ethics, and reflexivity in the practice of research; and is typically conducted at the margins of traditional disciplines.

Common to each of these approaches is the idea that feminist research involves something more than adding women and stirring or simply controlling for gender by means of a single variable. Feminist research requires a shift in how we approach research, but it does not require a focus on women, *per se*. Feminist research requires a feminist perspective, but feminist research might not focus primarily on gender. And certainly, feminist research needn't be produced by women. As Harding writes, "obviously, neither the ability nor the willingness to contribute to feminist understanding are sex-linked traits!" (1987, p. 11).

Feminist research, then, is not necessarily distinguished by the topic of research, nor by the sex, gender, or political affiliation of the researchers involved. Rather, feminist research is distinguished by *how* the research is done and, to some extent, by what is done with the research. What theoretical perspective(s) does the researcher bring to the research, and how does this inform her or his approach to doing the actual research—formulating questions, planning research design, interpreting results, disseminating information? Because there are multiple approaches to feminism and multiple varieties of feminism, there are also multiple approaches to feminist research.[i]

Feminist Theory and Survey Research

Despite feminist methodologists' broad understanding of what constitutes feminist research, many contemporary scholars—both feminists and otherwise—continue to see quantitative survey research as being at odds with feminist theory. This is true for a number of reasons. Within the social sciences, feminist scholars have rightly critiqued survey research for reducing gender to "sex"—a dichotomous variable[ii] that obscures the relationship between gender (which social scientists and feminist scholars typically consider to be socially based) and sex (which is typically understood as something more physiological).[iii]

Too often in survey research, gender (which becomes synonymous with sex) then appears to be a stable property of individuals ("She is female.")—rather than a "principle of social organization" (Stacey & Thorne, 1985, p. 307). Focusing on gender at the level of the individual, we lose sight of the processes through which gender is socially constructed and maintained. We also risk losing sight of how gender operates as a *social institution*—how gender "establishes the patterns of expectations for individuals" and "orders the social processes of everyday life" (Lorber, 1994, p. 1). A similar reductive process occurs with measures of race and ethnicity. As sociologist Tukufu Zuberi (in Zuberi & Bonilla-Silva, 2008, Introduction, p. 6) writes, "when we discuss the 'effect of race,' [in statistical models] we are less mindful of the larger social world in which the path to success or failure is influenced." Analyzing racial difference and inequality by means of a single dichotomous variable, we risk losing sight of the institutional dimensions of racial inequality (Pager & Shepherd, 2008; Zuberi, 2001). We also risk losing sight of the dynamic social processes that create racial groups and

---

[i] Naples (2003, pp. 3–4) makes a similar claim: "Since there are diverse feminist perspectives, it follows that there are different ways feminist researchers identify, analyze, and report 'data.'"

[ii] Dichotomous, or "dummy," variables are those that have two and only two options, such as "male" and "female," or, in attitudinal research, "agree" or "disagree." In statistical analyses, these are typically coded 0 and 1, though what numbers are assigned to what category makes no difference, so long as they are interpreted properly.

[iii] Increasingly, feminist scholars see *sex* itself as socially constructed. See, for example, Butler (1990), Kessler (1998), and Fausto-Sterling (2000).

maintain differences among them. In other words, we risk essentializing race and racial differences (Zuberi & Bonilla-Silva, 2008).

By understanding gender and race as social institutions, rather than as stable properties of individual people, we can see how culturally and historically specific ideas about gender are "built into the [other] major social organizations of society, such, as the economy, ideology, the family, and politics" (Lorber, 1994, p. 1). We can also see how gender is connected to the other major systems of inequality such, as race, nation, sexuality, and class.

Feminist scholars in the humanities have been largely critical of quantitative survey research, although their criticisms are often different from those described above. While feminist social scientists have critiqued quantitative survey research primarily on the basis of *method* (i.e., "gender as a variable"), critiques from the humanities focus more broadly on *methodology* and *epistemology* (the study of knowledge—what can be known? And who can know?). In this critique, the very foundations of social science are called into question. As Harding (1987, p. 182) points out, "scientific knowledge-seeking is supposed to be value-neutral, objective, dispassionate, disinterested, and so forth. It is supposed to be protected from political interests, goals, and desires (such as feminist ones) by the norms of science." And yet feminist research, by definition, has interests and values, for example, social justice and human rights. While Harding herself argues that these differences are not irreconcilable, others strongly disagree (e.g., Chafetz, 2004a).

In addition to these critiques, feminist standpoint theorists from both the humanities and social sciences have argued that quantitative research is limited in so far as it rarely takes into consideration the social and historical contexts in which it is produced. Quantitative research is often presented as value-free, objective, and disinterested. Rarely do quantitative scholars cast a critical eye on the processes through which research is produced and how the research production process may reflect (and even reproduce) social inequalities.

Feminist standpoint theorists, in contrast, have argued that knowledge about the social world is often structured by social inequalities (e.g., Hartsock, 1983/2003; Hill Collins, 1990/2000; Smith, 1974; Sprague, 2005; Valadez, 2001). Individuals who share particular social statuses or social locations often share meaningful experiences, which in turn can generate shared knowledge about the social world. If, however, in our scientific research, the voices and experiences of privileged groups are consistently represented but those of underprivileged groups are marginalized or excluded entirely, then the resulting knowledge claims are necessarily limited. Standpoint theorists emphasize the value in understanding all knowledge claims (whether they be made by privileged or underprivileged groups) as *partial* perspectives. For standpoint theorists, social science research is never value-free, objective, or disinterested—it is always produced from a particular perspective and within a particular context—nor should it aspire to be so. Rather, standpoint theorists embrace the idea that knowledge is socially situated and seek to produce and value knowledge grounded in subordinate, social positions.[iv]

Although feminist theory offers a number of important critiques of quantitative research techniques (and social science more generally), this does not necessarily mean that the two are fundamentally irreconcilable. In fact, quantitative research has been an important tool for understanding, documenting, and challenging gender inequalities and social inequalities more generally. Consider, for example, how quantitative research has helped to document feminist gains—and lingering inequalities—in higher education. Survey research shows us that in 1970, women represented 40% of college students enrolled in degree-granting institutions in the United States. By 2007, this percentage had increased to more than half (55%).[v] Fifty-seven percent of bachelor's degrees conferred in the 2000–2001 school year were awarded to women, up from 43% in 1969–1970.[vi] But despite these gains, women still earn only 20% of the bachelor's degrees awarded in the field of engineering and less than a third (28%) of the degrees conferred in computer and information sciences.[vii]

[iv] See also Hill Collins (2000), Haraway (1988, 1990), Hartsock (1983).

[v] Source: U.S. Department of Education, National Center for Education Statistics, Higher Education General Information Survey (HEGIS), Fall Enrollment in Colleges and Universities surveys, 1970 and 1980; 1990 through 2006 Integrated Postsecondary Education Data System, Fall Enrollment Survey (IPEDS-EF:90–99), and Spring 2001 through Spring 2007; and *Projections of Education Statistics to 2017.* U.S. Department of Commerce, Census Bureau, Current Population Survey (CPS), October, selected years, 1970 through 2007. (This table was prepared August 2008.) Retrieved March 3, 2010, from http://nces.ed.gov/programs/digest/d08/tables/dt08_190.asp

[vi] Source: U.S. Department of Education, National Center for Education Statistics, Higher Education General Information Survey (HEGIS), "Degrees and Other Formal Awards Conferred Survey;" and Integrated Postsecondary Education Data System, "Completions Survey" (IPEDS-C:01), 2000–01. Retrieved March 3, 2010, from http://nces.ed.gov/pubs2005/equity/figures.asp?PopUp=true&FigureNumber=K

[vii] Source: U.S. Department of Education, National Center for Education Statistics, Higher Education General Information Survey (HEGIS), Degrees and Other Formal Awards Conferred Survey; and Integrated Postsecondary Education Data System, Completions Survey (IPEDS-C:01), 2000–01. Retrieved March 3, 2010, from http://nces.ed.gov/pubs2005/equity/figures.asp?PopUp=true&FigureNumber=K

Quantitative analyses of the U.S. Census Bureau's Current Population Survey (CPS) have similarly helped feminists keep track of gendered economic inequalities. In March of 1964, the CPS revealed that the weekly wages of full-time, year-round women workers, aged 25 to 64, were 58% of what full-time, year-round men workers of the same age group earned.[viii] More than 4 decades later, the U.S. Census Bureau reported women's earnings had improved relative to men's, but, they noted, a significant wage gap remains. In 2008, women in the United States who worked full-time, year-round earned only 77% of what full-time, year-round men workers earned.[ix] Further, a recent report from the U.S. Bureau of Labor Statistics shows that the gender gap in earnings remains at every level of educational attainment: In the fourth quarter of 2009, the median weekly earning for men who were working full time but who had earned less than a high-school education was $686.[x] For women, the corresponding figure was $477, roughly 70% that of men's earnings. For men and women with bachelor's degree or higher, the weekly earnings for full-time workers were $1,896 and $1,384, respectively—a gender gap of 73%.

In addition to documenting material inequalities, quantitative survey research has been a valuable tool for documenting cultural beliefs about gender and how these beliefs have changed over time. Over the past several decades, the U.S.-based General Social Survey (GSS), for example, has regularly asked respondents whether they believed that "most men are better suited emotionally for politics than are most women." In 1974, nearly half of men agreed with this statement (47.6%). In 2010, 23.3% of men surveyed agreed. Attitudes have clearly changed since the 1970s, but with nearly one in four men still clinging to the belief that women are ill-suited for politics (and notably, nearly 1 in 5 women are also clinging to this belief!), women politicians and those aspiring to become politicians still face a tremendous obstacle. In another example, in 2010, the GSS also asked respondents about their views about balancing work and family. Strikingly, one out of three women surveyed (33.7%) and more than a third of men (39.1%) indicated that they agreed or strongly agreed with the statement that "it is much better for everyone involved if the man is

---

[viii] Explaining Trends in the Gender Wage Gap. June 1998. A Report by The Council of Economic Advisers. Retrieved February 21, 2010, from http://clinton4.nara .gov/textonly/WH/EOP/CEA/html/gendergap.html#2

[ix] Retrieved February 20, 2010, from http://www.census.gov/Press-Release/www/ releases/archives/income_wealth/014227.html

[x] This report was based on data collected in the fourth quarter of 2009. Source: Table 4. Retrieved from http://www.bls.gov/cps/earnings.htm#education

the achiever outside the home and the woman takes care of the home and family." Though stories in popular culture tell of women's advances leaving men in the dust, survey research presents an alternative, sobering view: Gender inequality persists.

Survey research has clearly played an important role in the fight for gender equality in education, work, and families. But quantitative analyses of survey research have been important tools for understanding other manifestations of sexism as well—including those beyond the realm of what we might consider "liberal" articulations of feminism. For example, quantitative survey research has been important for understanding and challenging a culture of violence against women. In particular, survey research has helped reframe debates about sexual assault so that *stranger rape* no longer occupies the forefront in discussions of violence against women. Survey research has shown us that women in the United States are more likely to be killed in their homes than in any other setting. The National Coalition Against Domestic Violence (NCADV) reports that "almost one-third of female homicide victims that are reported in police records are killed by an intimate partner."[xi] In addition, survey research has shown us that the vast majority (85%–90%) of victims of sexual assault on American college campuses know their assailants—sadly, about half of such incidents occur during a date.[xii] Survey research and quantitative data analysis more generally have also helped document changes in gender ideology and, relatedly, in cultural representations of men and women. Despite the much discussed "death of feminism" in the 1980s and 1990s, survey data analyzed by Bolzendahl and Myers (2004) and Huddy, Neely, and LaFay (2000) document increased support for feminist ideals over the past several decades.[xiii] Analyzing research from dozens of surveys across more than three decades, Huddy et al. (2000, pp. 316–317) conclude that support for the U.S. women's movement "shows no sign of diminishing in the 1990s" and that "[y]oung people remain staunch movement supporters" (see also Harnois, 2008; Peltola, Milkie, & Presser, 2004).

[xi] The NCADV fact sheet cites: Federal Bureau of Investigation, *Uniform Crime Reports*, Crime in the United States, 2000. (2001). NCADV fact sheet. Retrieved March 3, 2010, from http://www.ncadv.org/

[xii] Retrieved March 3, 2010, from http://www.ojp.usdoj.gov/nij/topics/crime/rape-sexual-violence/campus/know-attacker.htm

[xiii] Bolzendahl and Myers (2004, p. 760) conclude that feminist attitudes among women and men, "have continued to liberalize . . . with the exception of abortion attitudes, which have remained stable."

In brief, quantitative analyses of survey research have played an important role in helping to understand and challenge systems of inequality in many of its varied forms. As sociologist Christine Williams writes,

> quantitative analysis is necessary if feminists are to intervene in important political debates. . . . Sometimes we need numbers to present a compelling argument, to inspire activism, and to get things changed. . . . [W]e cannot and should not give up on the quantitative study of gender. (2006, p. 456)

Risman, Sprague, and Howard (1993, p. 608) sum it up nicely: "Some feminist questions demand quantitative answers."

While feminist critiques of quantitative research are numerous, feminist scholars have offered important critiques of (almost?) every kind of research in the social sciences as well as in the humanities and biological sciences. For example, feminist scholars have critiqued ethnography, participant observation, oral history, content analysis, literary criticism, experimental research, and medical trials, in addition to quantitative survey research. But rather than abandoning these approaches, many feminist scholars have sought to *improve* these techniques—and in many cases, to use them to different ends. For example, ethnographic research may, at one time, have been a tool of imperialism, but many anthropologists and sociologists today use ethnographic research to subvert neocolonialism and other systems of inequality, working *with* disempowered groups around the world to help achieve their goals (e.g., Booth, 2004; Hewamanne, 2008; Naples & Desai, 2002). Radical methodological critiques—whether they be feminist, postmodern, antiracist, and/or postcolonial—have not always advocated throwing the proverbial baby out with the bathwater; rather, they have often worked to transform and reappropriate these techniques. They have used these transformed techniques in combination with other approaches and have drawn post-positivistic conclusions about the social world.[xiv] As Risman (2001, p. 610) writes, "feminist [social science] scholarship expresses a commitment to science with and from a value position. This is a rejection of the belief in the possibility of value-free singular context-less scientific 'Truth,' but it is neither a rejection of all science nor an acceptance of relativism." From a post-positivist perspective, feminist scholars seek to identify the "cultural elements" that shape scientific inquiry, and to "figure out which of these cultural elements are at this particular historical moment advancing and which blocking the growth of knowledge" (Harding 1998, p. 145; see also Risman, 1993; Sprague & Zimmerman, 1989, 1993).

[xiv] Positivism emphasizes the promise and possibility of objectivity in science. As Sprague (2005, p. 32) writes, "positivism assumes that truth comes from eliminating the role of subjective judgments and interpretations."

My approach to feminist survey research builds on the feminist transformations and reappropriations described above. While many varieties of feminism can (and have) informed survey research, in this book, I highlight the implications of multiracial feminist theory for social science survey research. Though it is seldom employed in conjunction with survey research, multiracial feminist theory offers the grounds for the transformation, reappropriation, and post-positivist interpretation of survey research.

What is Multiracial Feminist Theory?

In their article, "Theorizing Difference From Multiracial Feminism," Maxine Baca Zinn and Bonnie Thornton Dill (1996) describe multiracial feminism as a broad-based theoretical perspective in which race, gender, class, sexuality, and nation are understood as *intersecting* systems of inequality. This idea of systems of inequality as intersecting with one another—*intersectionality*—is meant to suggest something beyond additive models of oppression that came before.[xv] While multiracial feminists acknowledge that many individuals are simultaneously disadvantaged by multiple systems of inequality (for example, racial minority women may face racism and sexism), they argue that additive models of inequality are insufficient for understanding the complexity of the social world. By examining systems of inequality as separate and distinct systems, additive models fail to address ways in which systems of inequality work "with and through each other" and influence the lives of all people, privileged and underprivileged alike (Baca Zinn & Thornton Dill, 1996, p. 326).

In contrast to those feminists who seek to understand gender in isolation from other systems of inequality, multiracial feminists explicitly locate the

---

[xv] As discussed in the preface, I use the language of "multiracial feminist theory" because it draws attention to the importance of race and feminism in the intellectual genealogy of contemporary "intersectional" scholarship. In addition, the term *multiracial feminist theory* draws attention to the importance of *theorizing* difference, as opposed to simply highlighting or "discovering" difference. As intersectionality becomes more mainstream, there is considerable risk of its becoming a "buzzword" (Davis, 2008) and in the process, risk of losing both its theoretical complexity and radical potential. The phrase "multiracial feminist theory" reminds us that differences must be theorized and that historically the most important intellectual work in this area has been done by women of color, that is, by multiracial feminists.

social construction of gender (and other systems of stratification) within a broader context of intersecting social hierarchies. These intersections take place at the level of the individual, where "people experience race, class, gender, and sexuality differently depending upon their social location in the structures of race, class, gender, and sexuality" (Baca Zinn & Thornton Dill, 1996, pp. 326–327). They also intersect at the institutional level, where, for example, systems of race, gender, class, and sexuality reinforce one another and are each built into our political, economic, and cultural institutions.[xvi]

Multiracial feminist theorists acknowledge that, in particular situations, any given social status or system of inequality may be more or less salient (e.g., Jordan, 1982/2003). But they refuse to designate one system of inequality as universally more significant than others, as the intersections of systems of inequality are both dynamic as well as "organized through diverse local realities" (Hill Collins, 1990/2000, p. 228; but see also Combahee River Collective, 1981; Jordan, 1982/2003; Weber, 2001). Multiracial feminists' refusal to privilege universally one system of inequality over others has resulted historically in *intersectional politics*—political movements and global and community activism—that similarly refuses a single-oppression framework (e.g., Berger, 2004; Combahee River Collective, 1981; Roth, 2004).

In addition to emphasizing the intersections of systems of inequality, multiracial feminists have emphasized the "relational nature of dominance and subordination" as well as women's agency. As Baca Zinn and Thornton Dill explain, "intersecting forms of domination produce *both* oppression *and* opportunity. At the same time that structures of race, class, and gender create disadvantages for women of color, they provide unacknowledged benefits for those who are at the top of these hierarchies—whites, members of the upper classes, and males" (Baca Zinn & Thornton Dill, 1996, p. 327; see also Baca Zinn, Hondagneu-Sotelo, & Messner, 2000/2007; Barkley Brown, 1992). Multiracial feminist theory focuses not only on *difference* and *particularity* but also on the relationships, inequalities, and social processes that help create and maintain these differences. This focus on the relationships that structure difference and inequality stands in stark contrast to "patchwork quilt" (Baca Zinn et al., 2000/2007) and "mosaic" models (May, 2010) of difference. In these latter approaches, difference and particularity are highlighted, but the social structures in which these differences are embedded remain unexplored.

[xvi] See Weber (2001) for an excellent discussion of how power relations intersect and are expressed simultaneously at the macro and micro levels.

In emphasizing *relationality*, multiracial feminism highlights the process through which differences are created and maintained.

For Baca Zinn and Thornton Dill, the final "distinguishing features" of multiracial feminism concern issues of methodology and accountability. They explain, "multiracial feminism encompasses wide-ranging methodological approaches, and like other branches of feminist thought, relies on varied theoretical tools as well" (1996, p. 328).[xvii] These theoretical and methodological approaches come from across the humanities and social sciences. However, since many of the central works of multiracial feminism were neither produced by "traditional" academics nor produced in traditional academic spaces, multiracial feminism underscores the need to engage with intellectual work outside of academia as well. Historically, structured inequalities of race, class, gender, and nation have worked to limit educational and career opportunities for women of color. These intersecting inequalities have limited women's ability to acquire prestigious positions within academia, and have also limited their ability to produce and publish scholarship in those outlets with the most academic legitimacy. As a result, many women of color intellectuals turned to nontraditional spaces to create and disseminate their work (and oftentimes, as in the case of Kitchen Table Press, they created these spaces in the process). As with feminist standpoint theorists, multiracial feminist theorists have drawn attention to how social locations help to shape knowledge; they have argued that "lived experiences . . . create alternative ways of understanding the social world and the experience of different groups . . . within it" (Baca Zinn & Thornton Dill, 1996, p. 328; see also Hill Collins, 1990/2000). Multiracial feminist scholarship embraces these alternative understandings, which have been marginalized within traditional scholarship and in some situations ignored completely.

Finally, in emphasizing the inequalities built into the knowledge production process, multiracial feminism raises the issue of accountability. In her essay "La Güera," Chicana feminist Cherríe Moraga writes, "so often the [white] women seem to feel no loss, no lack, no absence when women of color are not involved; therefore, there is little desire to change the situation" (1981/1983, p. 33). In her speech "The Master's Tools Will Never Dismantle the Master's House," Audre Lorde (1979/1984) makes a similar point. She calls attention to the dearth of "women of Color" represented

---

[xvii] See also Hancock (2007), who argues that an intersectional approach must be both empirical and theoretical and must draw from multiple methods.

at academic feminist conferences, and she challenges her audience to think critically about that situation:

> Why weren't other women of Color found to participate in this conference? Why were two phone calls to me considered a consultation? Am I the only possible source of names of Black feminists?
>
> In academic feminist circles, the answer to these questions is often, "We did not know who to ask." But that is the same evasion of responsibility, the same cop-out, that keeps Black women's art out of women's exhibitions, Black women's work out of feminist publications except for the occasional "Special Third World Women's Issue," and Black women's texts off your reading list. But as Adrienne Rich pointed out . . . white feminists have educated themselves about such an enormous amount over the past ten years, how come you haven't also educated yourselves about Black women and the differences between us—white and Black—when it is key to our survival as a movement? (1984, p. 113)

In her essay "Age, Race, Class, and Sex," Lorde writes of a similar phenomenon at work within the classroom:

> The literature of women of Color is seldom included in women's literature courses and almost never in other literature courses, nor in women's studies as a whole. All too often, the excuse given is that the literatures of women of Color can only be taught by Colored women, or that they are too difficult to understand. . . . I have heard this argument presented by white women of otherwise quite clear intelligence, women who seem to have no trouble at all teaching and reviewing work that comes out of the vastly different experiences of Shakespeare, Molière, Dostoyefsky, and Aristophanes. Surely there must be some other explanation. (1984, p. 117)

Lorde and Moraga highlight the need for privileged groups to educate themselves about issues of difference and inequality and about groups who are different from themselves. They push women to think critically about what has become routine, normative, and taken for granted. They push women to take responsibility for the role they play in maintaining inequality and to hold themselves accountable to something beyond what is expected.

Multiracial Feminist Theory and Survey Research

The question of accountability—not, To whom are we accountable? but rather, To whom do we *choose* to hold ourselves accountable?—is an important one for feminist research, as well as teaching and activism.[xviii] In "traditional" social science research, scholars are typically held accountable to discipline-specific expectations: What questions are the most central or important? Which theorists are important and thus worth reading and citing? What methods are typically used? How long is a typical article? Is it appropriate to use the first person? and so forth. Multiracial feminist theories push scholars to think critically about these norms. The goal is not to denigrate research grounded in traditional academic disciplines but rather to understand how disciplinary norms structure the knowledge production process and the resulting knowledge claims. Only then can we develop alternative research strategies that bring into focus what previous research has obscured.

As we will see in greater detail in the next chapter, disciplinary norms structure the social science research process, rendering some questions, theories, methods, and interpretations more legitimate and others less so. In so doing, these norms can perpetuate inequalities already built into the system. As sociologist Barrie Thorne (2006, p. 477) explains, disciplines "discipline, in the positive sense of providing training, honing methodological skills, and sustaining communities of practice. But, they also enforce conventions, sustain hierarchies and mechanisms of exclusion, and police boundaries (as in the cursing phrase 'that's not sociology!')." If convention dictates that class inequality is more "central" than race or gender, as has historically been the case in the field of sociology, then critical race and feminist theories are relegated to the margins and with them the experiences of racial minorities and women. If convention dictates that samples composed mostly of middle-class, white American college students are sufficient for making general claims about the social world, then the experiences of lower- and working-class, racial minority, and international students—not to mention older, nonstudent populations—will similarly remain hidden. In

---

[xviii] In her recent article "Be longing: Toward a feminist politics of relation," Aimee Carrillo Rowe (2005), asks feminists to reconsider the politics of location, as a way of thinking. She asks, "What gets left out when the conditions and effects of belonging to a 'location' are assumed as a starting point for our theorizing?" (2005, p. 15). She urges the reader to reframe the question, "To whom are we accountable?"—a question that takes the link between social location and accountability as a given (e.g., I am a woman, and so I am accountable to women; I am a sociologist, and so I am accountable to sociologists). Instead, she suggests, we might ask, "To whom do we *choose* to be accountable?" Accountability need not stem solely from our particular social locations. We can, she suggests, choose to hold ourselves accountable to a broader political or intellectual community, and doing so often involves building relationships across diverse communities.

emphasizing the value of diverse methodological approaches and theoretical perspectives, multiracial feminism advocates expanding the intellectual and political communities to which we choose to hold ourselves accountable. Doing things as they are typically done is simply not enough.

As Berger and Guidroz write of the "intersectional approach," multiracial feminism emphasizes "border-crossing," and "challenges traditional ways of framing research inquiries, questions, and methods" (2009, p. 7). What I hope to show here, though, is that multiracial feminist theory offers more than a challenge to—and more than a critique of—survey research. Multiracial feminism offers an alternate approach for doing survey research. It emphasizes difference and inequality, relationality, and the circumstances under which the research itself is produced—as Harding (1987, p. 183) calls it, the "context of discovery." As I show in the following chapters, multiracial feminism offers the grounds for transformation and reappropriation, interdisciplinary border crossing, and post-positivist interpretations of survey research.

Organization of the Book

In what follows, I hope to show the promise of a multiracial feminist approach to survey research. Three themes in particular stand out. First, multiracial feminist scholarship offers substantive insights into the social world that have been underused by survey researchers. Second, multiracial feminist theorizing offers survey researchers a number of analytic interventions that can bring greater complexity and nuance to social science research. And third, by highlighting difference, inequality, relationality, and the context of discovery, a multiracial feminist perspective can help survey researchers increase the quality of social science research.

The next chapter provides an overview of contemporary feminist survey research from across the social sciences and within women's and gender studies. I analyze a sample of more than 50 quantitative articles published in five feminist journals in the past two decades and investigate the extent of disciplinary boundaries in scholars' theoretical perspectives, as well as in their survey tools and their analytic techniques. While interdisciplinarity is a key theme in multiracial feminist theory and feminist theory more generally, feminist survey research remains largely structured by disciplinary boundaries. And while scholars in each discipline have engaged with some aspects of multiracial feminist theory, the majority of quantitative survey research does not. I conclude by considering how disciplinary boundaries might work to constrain the development of a multiracial feminist approach, and return to this idea in each of the following chapters.

What would it mean, in practical terms, to bring a multiracial feminist, or *intersectional* framework to survey research? In Chapters 3 to 5, I demonstrate several approaches for bringing a multiracial feminist framework to social science survey research. I focus on issues of meaning, measurement and modeling, and seek to show how multiracial feminist theorizing can inform each aspect of survey research. Chapter 3 focuses on sexism, Chapter 4 on racism, and Chapter 5 on feminism. I begin each chapter by discussing the contributions of prior survey research in these areas. My goal is not to denigrate prior research but rather to highlight its importance for social justice, social change, and social theory. I then guide the reader through some of the limitations of this research. My focus is on the hidden assumptions of survey instruments and multivariate models. For example, what kinds of questions do we ask when we want to gauge women's experiences with sexism? Do our measures make sense for women of different ages, racial groups, and socioeconomic classes? Imagine that we were to design a new survey, focusing just on young women's experiences. What survey questions would be most relevant? Would any of the measures be inappropriate? What additional questions would we ask? What literature would we consult to help us answer these questions? How are differences represented in our statistical models? And what assumptions of sameness are challenged when we begin from a multiracial feminist perspective? Finally, what analytic strategies are available for multiracial feminist analyses of survey research?

Throughout these chapters, I explore the feminist theories that I have found most valuable for answering these questions. As we think through these and other questions, we begin to see how our measures are constructed with an eye toward the experiences of particular groups. Often, our measures work best for groups that are more privileged. Often, our measures and our models help obscure the experiences of those who are already marginalized.

In the concluding chapter, I bring together the methodological findings from the previous chapters and outline six considerations for thinking about survey research from a multiracial feminist perspective. A multiracial feminist approach is useful not only for survey research on racism, sexism, and feminism but also for many kinds of survey research and for social science more generally.

2

(Inter)Disciplinarity in Feminist Survey Research

"Feminist ideas have been a trans-disciplinary force in the academy with the potential, along with allied political and intellectual movements, to reconfigure knowledge rather than simply inserting new enclaves within each province of the 19th century intellectual universe."

~Judith Stacey and Barrie Thorne (1996, p. 1)

Introduction

As explained in the previous chapter, early approaches to feminist research in the social sciences aimed to transform traditional academic disciplines. Feminist scholars sought to centralize women's issues within the humanities, social sciences, and biological sciences. They introduced new questions and considered new sources of information (e.g., Lerner, 1979; Smith, 1974; Stacey & Thorne, 1985). They challenged gender bias and sexism in the research process and worked to give intellectual legitimacy to a variety of issues related to women and gender more broadly.

Though these struggles continue, feminist scholars today increasingly advocate for feminist transformations that move beyond traditional academic boundaries. *Interdisciplinarity* is thought to be an important feature of feminist scholarship for a number of reasons. At the most basic level, because the roots of feminist theory span multiple fields of inquiry, fully engaging with this research requires scholars to cross disciplinary boundaries. Moreover, because feminist theories emerge not only from academic scholarship, but also from politics and activism, engaging with feminist theories often involves traveling beyond the boundaries of academia as well.

On a more theoretical level, contemporary feminist scholars have suggested that interdisciplinarity is an important tool for identifying and critiquing the power structures embedded in the knowledge production process. For many contemporary feminists, the promise of women's studies lies not in its ability to offer a comprehensive understanding of "women" or, for that matter, "gender," but rather in its ability to embrace contradiction and multiplicity. As Robyn Wiegman argues, rather than demanding "referential coherence" within women's studies (a disciplined approach), we might "define the impossibility of coherence as the central problematic and most important animating feature of feminism as a knowledge formation in the contemporary academy" (2002, p. 107). Women's studies as a critical project, particularly in its humanistic manifestations, is centrally concerned with contesting taken-for-granted and hegemonic knowledge claims, and interdisciplinary scholarship is a key tool for doing so. As Vivian May (2002, p. 134–135) writes, contemporary women's studies as "an area of inquiry and knowledge production" . . . "resists closure, invites conversation, and promotes a reflexive capacity for 'ongoing reinterpretation' and accountability."[i]

In addition to the reasons described above, interdisciplinarity is a particularly important feature of multiracial feminist scholarship. In "Theorizing Difference From Multiracial Feminism," Baca Zinn and Thornton Dill (1996, p. 324) explain that multiracial feminist scholarship has, from its inception, been an interdisciplinary project.

> "U.S. multiracial feminism encompasses several emergent perspectives developed primarily by women of color: African Americans, Latinas, Asian Americans, and Native Americans, women whose analyses are shaped by their unique perspectives as 'outsiders within'—marginal intellectuals whose social locations provide them with a particular perspective on self and society."

Audre Lorde (1984), Patricia Hill Collins (1990/2000), and Barbara Christian (1995) take idea this one step further. They note that historically the intersecting inequalities of race, class, and gender have worked to deny educational and career opportunities to women of color. This structured inequality has worked to keep women of color from acquiring prestigious

---

[i] In speaking of "ongoing reinterpretation," May is drawing from Lorraine Code, *Rhetorical spaces: Essays on gendered locations* (New York: Routledge, 1995), p. 135.

positions within academia and has thus limited their ability to produce and publish scholarship in those outlets with the most academic legitimacy. As a result, women of color intellectuals have often turned to nontraditional spaces to create and disseminate their work.

Multiracial feminist theorists highlight the ways in which "knowledge" is structured by inequalities of race, gender, and class. It is not simply that some voices are given more credibility or legitimacy than others, but that some groups have had more access to the resources (e.g., academic credentials, time, administrative support, sabbaticals, work-related benefits, and money) required to produce "academically legitimate" knowledge. Because multiracial feminist theorizing has been frequently produced outside of "academic spaces," engaging fully with multiracial feminism requires contemporary scholars to travel across both disciplinary and *academic* boundaries. Social scientists must be open-minded enough to see "theory" and "hypotheses" in nontraditional spaces—in essays and poetry, for example—for key insights into the social world are not found only in peer-reviewed academic journal articles and monographs (Christian, 1995; Hill Collins, 2000; Lorde, 1984).

There is a broader social justice issue at stake here as well: If we accept that the knowledge production process has been historically organized around inequalities of gender, race, and class, then to uncritically perpetuate knowledge-based hierarchies is to perpetuate those systems of inequality built into the knowledge production process.[ii] Finger and Rosner (2001, p. 499) write, "Women's studies was born out of an interdisciplinary mission, a commitment to challenge the limits of the disciplinary production of knowledge, and to expose the blind spots and structures of exclusion within the disciplinary system."[iii] Insofar as academic feminism is concerned with social justice, feminist scholars must consider how social inequalities have historically shaped the knowledge–production process and how these inequalities might continue to do so today.

(Inter)Disciplinarity in Feminist Survey Research

While interdisciplinarity is an important theme in multiracial feminism, and in feminist theory more broadly, few studies have systematically investigated the extent to which feminist research is characterized by interdisciplinarity.[iv]

[ii] See Kyungwon Hong (2008).

[iii] See also Hawkesworth (2006, p. 3), who writes, "Pushing against that which is most taken for granted, feminist inquiry probes absences, silences, omissions, and distortions in order to challenge common sense understandings that often rely upon evidence taken from a narrow sample of the human population."

[iv] For exception, see Allen and Kitch (1998).

Many have argued that knowledge produced from within narrow disciplinary boundaries is limited, but it can be difficult to pin down precisely how disciplinary structures shape the resulting knowledge claims. How do the norms of sociological research differ from those in psychology, for example, and how might our methodological choices constrain both our possible conclusions and the possibility of a multiracial feminist approach?

In this chapter, I assess the level of interdisciplinarity in contemporary feminist survey research, and explore how these boundaries constrain our conclusions about contemporary feminism. I begin by investigating the extent of interdisciplinary dialogue among feminist survey researchers, and then I assess disciplinary differences in method. I find that, within survey research, disciplinary boundaries continue to structure both feminist dialogue *and* feminist research methods. And in the absence of interdisciplinary dialogue, continued reliance on narrow disciplinary practices reinscribes the "blind spots and structures of exclusion" (Finger & Rosner, 2001) associated with any particular research method. This process of reinscription, I argue, has helped to deter the emergence of an intersectional or "multiracial feminist" approach to survey research in the social sciences.

Finding Feminist Survey Research

To assess the extent of interdisciplinarity in feminist survey research and to clarify the relationship between (inter)disciplinarity and multiracial feminist research, I first needed a good sample of contemporary feminist survey research. To find this sample, I turned to those journals I thought most likely to publish interdisciplinary feminist survey research: *Women & Politics (W&P), Gender & Society (G&S), Psychology of Women Quarterly (PWQ), National Women's Studies Association (NWSA) Journal* (recently renamed *Feminist Formations*), and *Signs*. Each of these is an important peer-reviewed, scholarly feminist journal, and each has published survey research on feminism over the past two decades.[v]

---

[v] *Gender & Society, Psychology of Women Quarterly*, and *Women & Politics* are the flagship "feminist" journals within sociology, psychology, and political science, respectively, and each of these fields relies heavily (though not exclusively) on survey research. The NWSA Journal (which was itself renamed *Feminist Formations* in 2009) is the flagship journal of the National Women's Studies Association, and claims to publish "the most up-to-date, interdisciplinary, multicultural feminist scholarship linking feminist theory with teaching and activism." According to its website (http://www.journals.uchicago.edu/page/signs/brief.html), *Signs: Journal of Women in Culture and Society* publishes "pathbreaking articles of interdisciplinary interest addressing gender, race, culture, class, nation, and/or sexuality either as central focuses or as constitutive analytics and symposia engaging comparative, interdisciplinary perspectives from around the globe to analyze concepts and topics of import to feminist scholarship." Each of the journals has published quantitative survey research in the past.

The former three journals are each affiliated with a social science disciplines—political science, sociology, and psychology—respectively and they regularly publish quantitative research. *Signs* and *NWSA Journal* typically publish qualitative, humanistic scholarship but occasionally publish quantitative survey research. I include these latter two journals in my analysis, because, unlike the former three journals, *Signs* and *NWSA Journal* are affiliated primarily with Women's Studies as a field of inquiry and both are explicitly interdisciplinary.

My analysis of these five journals does not, of course, represent all of feminist research, nor does it represent all of contemporary feminist survey research. Rather, the articles included in these five journals represent what I believe to be a "best case scenario" for interdisciplinary multiracial feminist survey research. Each of the journals is explicitly oriented toward feminism, each has published social science survey research, and, with the exception of *PWQ*, each explicitly welcomes article submissions from a variety of disciplines on its webpage. My assumption is that collectively these five journals represent the space where an interdisciplinary multiracial feminist approach to survey research is most likely to exist. To the extent that feminist survey research is characterized by interdisciplinarity and a multiracial feminist approach, we should find evidence of these attributes in the pages of these five journals.

Analytic Strategy

My analysis begins by examining each of the articles published in these five journals from 1988 to 2008 (inclusive). Within these journals, I found 56 articles that relied on survey research to investigate "feminism" or "feminists," and these articles form the basis of my analysis.[vi] As discussed in the previous chapter, feminist research need not focus on feminism, and I do not mean to suggest that, because of their focus, these articles are intrinsically more feminist than others in the journals. Rather, by limiting my analysis to articles that investigate feminism and that appear in feminist-oriented journals, this selection process increases the chances of finding interdisciplinarity in feminist survey research. In addition, by limiting my analysis to research on a particular topic, in this case feminism, I am better able to highlight the theoretical and methodological differences across disciplines.

[vi] I used a variety of databases, including Wiley Interscience, JStor, and Project Muse, to find articles that included "feminist(s)" or "feminism(s)" in the title. Collectively, these searches produced hundreds of articles, which I examined to determine whether they used survey research to analyze feminism.

Next, I investigate where feminist survey research is published and by whom it is produced. Is feminist survey research found more in some journals than in others? And is it produced by scholars in one discipline more than others? I find, somewhat surprisingly that the answer to both of these questions is 'yes'. Following this overview, I investigate the extent to which feminist researchers engage in interdisciplinary dialogue. Whom do survey researchers consult (i.e., cite) when theorizing and analyzing feminist issues? To what extent do disciplinary boundaries shape the architecture of citation networks?

My investigation of citation networks reveals that, despite claims of inter-disciplinarity, disciplinary boundaries continue to structure dialogue among feminist survey researchers. In the last portion of my analysis, I consider the link between disciplinary dialogues and disciplinary methods. What methodological approaches do survey researchers bring to their analyses of feminism? Which groups and which varieties of feminism are central to their analyses, and which are marginal? I conclude by suggesting that disciplinary boundaries structure both methodological and theoretical approaches, which together limit the possibility for a multiracial feminist approach.

Is Feminist Dialogue Structured by Disciplinary Boundaries? Assessing Citation Patterns

Table 2.1 presents an overview of the articles included in the sample. Of the 56 articles that employ survey research to analyze feminism, the major-ity (32) were published in *Psychology of Women Quarterly*. *Women & Politics* and *Gender & Society* also each published a significant number

Table 2.1   Overview of Contemporary Feminist Survey Research in Five Journals, 1989 to 2008.

Field	Journal Name	Number of Articles in Sample	Number of Articles With Author(s) From Same Field*
Psychology	*Psychology of Women Quarterly*	32	31
Political Science	*Women & Politics*	10	10
Sociology	*Gender & Society*	9	7
Women's Studies	*Signs*	3	1
Women's Studies	*NWSA Journal*	2	1

Note: *For *Women & Politics*, this category includes the fields of political science, government, and public affairs.

(10 and 9, respectively), while *Signs* and *NWSA Journal* each published only a handful. In almost all cases, the authors represented in the sample published in journals associated with their own disciplines. Though the sub-sample of women's studies articles is much smaller than contributions from the other fields, *NWSA Journal* and *Signs* stand out as publishing a high proportion of authors whose home discipline is outside of women's studies. Taken as a whole, it appears that survey research on feminism is more likely to be produced by psychologists than it is by scholars in other fields. I note here, however, that direct comparisons across these journals are not as straightforward as at first they may appear. Because the number of articles within each journal and the number of journal issues per year differ, journals that publish more articles per year are in a better position to publish higher numbers of articles using survey research to understand feminism.

My analysis continues by investigating dialogue among feminist research-ers within and across disciplines. I focus on the sample of articles described above and ask, first, Who are authors citing?, and second, By whom are authors cited? Table 2.2 presents answers to these questions in broad strokes. Reading across the first row, we see that, taken together, articles from *PWQ* referenced other articles in the sample (including other *PWQ* articles) sixty-five times.[vii] Fifty-eight of these citations (89.2%) connected *PWQ* articles to other articles from *PWQ*. The nine articles from *Gender*

Table 2.2   Description of Citation Networks Within and Across Fields.

	Number of Within-Sample Citations (Outgoing) (A)	Number of Within-Discipline Citations (B)	Percentage of Citations Within Discipline	Number of Times Articles Were Cited (Incoming) (C)
Psychology of Women Quarterly (32)	65	58	89.2%	61
Gender & Society (9)	14	7	50.0%	15
Women & Politics (10)	13	13	100%	22
Signs / NWSA Journal (5)	6	0	0%	0

[vii] I want to emphasize here that this number represents connections between articles. If one particular article in the sample cites another in the sample three times throughout the course of the article, I code this exactly the same as if there were only one citation. My measures indicate only whether there is a connection among articles, not the "strength" of that connection.

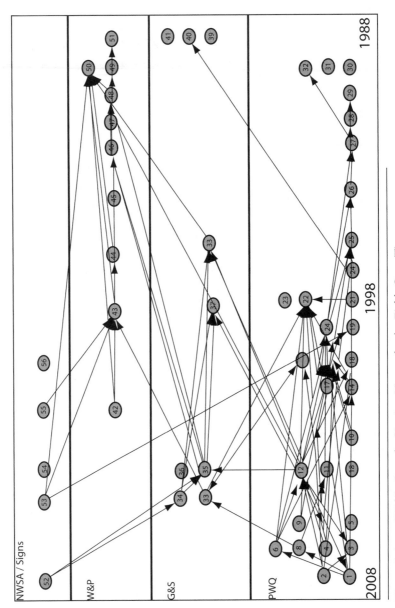

Figure 2.1   Within-Sample Citation Networks, by Field, Over Time.

& *Society* together cited 14 articles in the sample, but half of these citations were to other articles published in *Gender & Society*. Articles from *Women & Politics* together made 13 references to articles within the sample, but all of these citations were to other *Women & Politics* articles.

Column (C) represents the number of times that journal articles were cited by other articles within the sample (including articles within the same field) and is thus an indicator of journal impact within the realm of feminist survey research. Within the sample we find articles published in *Psychology of Women Quarterly* cited by other articles in the sample a total of 61 times. The nine articles published in *Gender & Society* were cited by other articles in the sample a total of fifteen times, and the ten articles published in *Women & Politics* were cited by other articles in the sample a total of twenty-two times.

Figure 2.1 represents a more complex picture of the architecture of citation networks, showing the connections among individual articles by discipline, over time. Each circle represents one of the articles in the sample. The bottom portion of the figure displays the 32 articles published in *Psychology of Women Quarterly*. The section above displays articles from *Gender & Society*, and above that are articles from *Women & Politics*. The topmost section represents articles from both the *NWSA Journal* and *Signs*. Articles are ordered chronologically, with most recent articles presented on the left and earlier articles toward the right. Articles that were published in the same year are stacked on top of one another (as in the case of articles 1, 2, and 52).

Each arrow in Figure 2.1 represents a citation linking one article in the sample to another. Because the articles are ordered chronologically, all of the arrows point to the right (articles are citing articles that were published earlier or, in a few cases, in the same year). Each arrow begins from an article that cites another in the sample, and points to the article being cited. So looking at the bottom left-hand corner, we see article 1 (published in *PWQ* in 2008) cites articles 3, 5, 6 (in *PWQ*) and also article 33 in *G&S* (in addition to other articles in the sample).

While visually overwhelming at first, this figure provides a visual representation of the architecture of citation networks across the sample. It also illustrates some interesting patterns. First, the majority of the articles are clustered in the bottom fourth of the figure, showing that the majority of the articles in the sample were published in *PWQ*. Second, arrows connecting articles are most dense in the bottom portion of this figure, suggesting that most of the citation networks in the sample connect *PWQ* articles with other *PWQ* articles. We can assess cross-journal and within-journal citations by comparing the number of arrows that cross the horizontal disciplinary boundaries with the number arrows that do not. For example, all of the arrows that originate from within *Women & Politics* are connected to other *Women & Politics* articles. On the other hand, a number of arrows originating from other journals point to (and thus cite) *Women & Politics* articles. The two women's studies journals present the opposite situation: None of the articles is cited by another in the sample, though three of the five women's studies articles together cite articles from the three other journals. If we take a step back and examine the larger picture, then we see three relatively horizontal clusters of arrows—arrows connecting *PWQ, G&S,* and *W&P* articles to other articles within their own disciplines. Dialogue among feminist survey researchers thus appears to be structured largely by disciplinary boundaries.

Presenting the citation networks in this way illustrates one additional important pattern: articles within the sample are cited at different rates. Some articles (e.g., 31, 41, 42, and 56) are not cited at all by others in the sample, while others (22 and 50) are cited more than 10 times within the sample. Most articles fall somewhere in between. Comparing citation networks in this way gives us a sense of the relative impact that individual articles have had within feminist survey research.[viii] It shows us that when survey researchers are researching and writing about feminism, they consult some articles and some academic journals more than others. Most importantly, researchers' choice of which articles to consult is structured by disciplinary boundaries.

Are Feminist Methods Structured by Disciplinary Boundaries? Assessing Survey Research Methods

My investigation of citation networks within survey research suggests that disciplinary boundaries continue to structure the dialogue among feminist researchers. But to what extent do disciplinary dialogues influence the research process? And how might the persistence of disciplinary practices, in combination with disciplinary-based dialogue, constrain our research findings and conclusions? To answer these questions, I analyze the methodological approaches used by feminist survey researchers.

Within the sample of 56 articles described above, there are three broad methodological approaches to analyzing feminism. The first approach uses large-scale survey data from pre-existing data sets to analyze feminism and typically measures feminism with a small number of survey items. In the second

---

[viii] It is important to note that articles published in very recent years are disadvantaged with this measure of impact, since little time has passed since their publication. Thus, there is less opportunity for subsequently published articles to cite their research. Note, too, that some of the connections in this figure represent authors citing their own research. Sometimes this takes place within the same journal and sometimes across journals.

approach scholars design their own survey instruments (or modify those of others) and administer them to smaller local samples. If feminism is at the heart of these studies, scholars typically include a large number (even dozens) of survey questions designed to measure respondents' beliefs and behaviors. Scholars who are primarily interested in the relationship between feminism and some other social or psychological phenomenon, however, generally rely on fewer measures of feminism. A third approach, less common than the other two, uses survey research to investigate feminism within a specific group of people ("judges and attorneys" [Martin, Reynolds, & Keith, 2002] or "Daytonian women" [Runyan & Wenning, 2004]), with no specific claims as to the generalizability of their measures or findings. The methodological characteristics of each approach are summarized in Table 2.3.

The first approach described above, which analyzes general survey data from large national samples, is found most frequently in *Women & Politics* and *Gender & Society*. Within the sample of articles explored here, half of the articles in each of these journals rely on this approach. Cook's (1989) study, "Measuring Feminist Consciousness" (article 50 in Figure 2.1), is among the earliest articles in the sample, and it is also the most heavily cited *Women & Politics* article in the sample of articles I examined. Her article analyzes data from the 1972, 1976, 1980, and 1984 American National Election Studies (ANES) to explore "politicized feminist consciousness" among women. The ANES consists of national surveys of the American electorate in election years, and it includes information about political participation and affiliations, public opinion, and a host of sociodemographic characteristics.[ix] It is a widely used survey in political science; four of the articles in *W&P* rely on data from the ANES, as does one study in *G&S* and one in *PWQ*.

In her analysis of the ANES, Cook (1989) uses a statistical technique called *factor analysis* to develop a measure of feminist consciousness that has two dimensions: (1) individuals' beliefs about "gender roles" (e.g., Should women have an equal role with men in running business, industry, and government, or is women's place in the home?) and (2) a "feeling thermometer" of the "women's liberation movement." (A feeling thermometer measures how "warm" or "cool" respondents feel toward a particular group or issue.) After developing this model, Cook uses multivariate regression analyses to determine which demographic factors are associated with a feminist consciousness. She then explores whether feminist consciousness, as she has measured it, is related to a variety of "feminist issues." She notes that there

---

[ix] For more information about the American National Election Studies see http://www.electionstudies.org/

Table 2.3   Methodological Characteristics of Three Types of Feminist Survey Research.

Disciplinary Affiliation	Data Analysis	Sample Size	Characteristics of Sample	"Feminist" Measures	Benefits for Multiracial Feminist Research
Political Science and Sociology	Secondary	Large	Very diverse Often nationally representative	Few in number Emphasis on "liberal feminism"	Diversity of sample Potential to compare groups within a single analysis
Psychology	Primary	Medium	Somewhat diverse Large reliance on university populations	Ranging from few to many in number Can include a broad range of "feminisms" within and across articles	Potential diversity of measures Potential to assess complexity of feminism and its relation to a variety of social-psychological factors
Women's and Gender Studies	Primary	Small	Little diversity within, but significant diversity across, samples	Few in number Includes a broad range of "feminisms" across articles	Potential diversity of measures Potential to assess complexity of feminism within a particular context

is "a divergence of opinions among activist feminists" (p. 83), but suggests that "most [feminists] have strongly supported the Equal Rights Amendment (ERA), and to a lesser extent abortion rights" (pp. 83–84). In addition, she suggests that "women with a politicized feminist consciousness [should] blame the system rather than women for existing inequalities" (p. 84).

In contrast to the first approach described above, many of the articles published in *Psychology of Women Quarterly* rely on survey data from smaller, more local samples, but also use much more numerous and diverse measures of feminist attitudes and identity. In what is perhaps the most extreme instance of this phenomenon, psychologist Nancy M. Henley and her colleagues (Henley, Meng, O'Brien, McCarthy, & Sockloskie, 1998) draw from "feminist writings exemplifying the different theoretical positions, from writings on feminist theories and theorists, and from eighteen in-depth interviews" to develop "a scale to measure the diversity of feminist attitudes" (p. 322). Henley et al.'s article (article 22 in Figure 2.1), draws on ten measures for each of six gender perspectives: gender-conservativism, liberal feminism, radical feminism, socialist feminism, and cultural feminism, as well as women of color feminism. The authors also developed an 18-item subscale to measure feminist or gender-conservative behaviors (e.g., "I use 'she' rather than 'he' generically, that is, to refer to an unknown person"). Table 2.4 presents the questions included in Henley et al.'s (1998) Feminist Perspectives Scale, arranged by subscale.

To test the validity and reliability of their measures, Henley et al. (1998) collected and analyzed data from several different samples. For the first portion of their study, their sample consisted of 117 respondents of mixed gender (92 from the "introductory psychology subject pool" and 25 women from an advanced women's studies seminar at a West Coast university; 82% of the sample respondents were between the ages of 18–22). The second portion of the study combined data from three different samples. The first consisted of 84 students from the same West Coast university (69 from the psychology subject pool and fifteen graduate students in a psychology of gender course); the second sample consisted of 94 people who were waiting in line to see a taping of the Arsenio Hall Show; the third sample consisted of another 166 respondents from the same introductory psychology subject pool. The third portion of their study used factor analyses to investigate the relationship among attitudinal items. In this portion, they included an additional 259 students (197 from the same subject pool and 62 from a psychology of women class at a West Coast liberal arts college).

The third general approach I found uses survey research to understand feminism as it relates to one specific group of people. Authors from this perspective emphasize the particularity of their sample; article titles often clearly identify the group being researched; and authors make few claims as to the generalizability of their findings. Indeed, to the contrary, authors often explicitly state that their conclusions are *not* generalizable to a broader population. Scholars who use this approach employ a wide range of measures to assess feminism, including self-identification as feminist (e.g., Runyan & Wenning, 2004), evaluation of the women's movement (e.g., Gruber & Bjorn, 1988), participation in feminist organizations and

Table 2.4   Feminist Perspectives Scale Items, Arranged by Subscale.

Conservative Perspective:

---

1. Given the way that men are, women have a responsibility not to arouse them by their dress and actions.

4. Women should not be direct participants in government because they are too emotional.

13. A man's first responsibility is to obtain economic success, while his wife should care for the family's needs.

17. Homosexuals need to be rehabilitated into normal members of society.

23. The breakdown of the traditional family structure is responsible for the evils in our society.

36. It is a man's right and duty to maintain order in his family by whatever means necessary.

38. The world is a more attractive place because women pay attention to their appearance and smiles.

47. Women should not be assertive like men because men are the natural leaders on earth.

53. Using "he" for "he or she" is convenient and harmless to men and women.

59. Heterosexuality is the only natural sexual preference.

Liberal Feminist Perspective:

5. Whether one chooses a traditional or alternative family form should be a matter of personal choice.

6. People should define their marriage and family roles in ways that make them feel most comfortable.

7. The government is responsible for making sure that all women receive an equal chance at education and employment.

22. The availability of adequate child care is central to a woman's right to work outside the home.

24. Homosexuality is not a moral issue, but rather a question of liberty and freedom of expression.

27. Social change for sexual equality will best come about by acting through federal, state, and local government.

33. Legislation is the best means to ensure a woman's choice of whether or not to have an abortion.

42. Women should try to influence legislation in order to gain the right to make their own decisions and choices.

52. Women should have the freedom to sell their the sexual services.

60. Men need to be liberated from oppressive sex role stereotypes as much as women do.

(Continued)

Table 2.4   (continued)

Radical Feminist Perspective:

2. Pornography exploits female sexuality and degrades all women.

15. Using "man" to mean both men and women is one of many ways sexist language destroys women's existence.

16. Sex role stereotypes are only one symptom of the larger system of patriarchal power, which is the true source of women's subordination.

18. The workplace is organized around men's physical, economic, and sexual oppression of women.

19. Men's control over women forces women to be the primary caretakers of children.

29. Men use abortion laws and reproductive technology to control women's lives.

34. Men prevent women from becoming political leaders through their control of economic and political institutions.

46. Marriage is a perfect example of men's physical, economic, and sexual oppression of women.

48. Romantic love brainwashes women and forms the basis for their subordination.

55. Rape is ultimately a powerful tool that keeps women in their place, subservient to and terrorized by men.

Socialist Feminist Perspective:

10. Capitalism and sexism are primarily responsible for the increased divorce rate and general breakdown of families.

20. Making women economically dependent on men is capitalism's subtle way of encouraging heterosexual relationships.

25. A socialist restructuring of businesses and institutions is necessary for women and people of color to assume equal leadership with White men.

31. Romantic love supports capitalism by influencing women to place men's emotional and economic needs first.

39. The way to eliminate prostitution is to make women economically equal to men.

41. Capitalism hinders a poor woman's chance to obtain adequate prenatal medical care or an abortion.

45. It is the capitalist system which forces women to be responsible for child care.

54. All religion is like a drug to people and is used to pacify women and other oppressed groups.

56. Capitalism forces most women to wear feminine clothes to keep a job.

58. The personalities and behaviors of "women" and "men" in our society have developed to fit the needs of advanced capitalism.

(Continued)

Table 2.4   (continued)

Cultural Feminist Perspective:

9. Prostitution grows out of the male culture of violence and male values of social control.

11. Replacing the word "God" with "goddess" will remind people that the deity is not male.

14. Men should follow women's lead in religious matters, because women have a higher regard for love and peace than men.

28. Putting women in positions of political power would bring about new systems of government that promote peace.

30. Traditional notions of romantic love should be replaced with ideas based on feminine values of kindness and concern for all people.

32. By not using sexist and violent language, we can encourage peaceful social change.

35. Beauty is feeling one's womanhood through peace, caring, and nonviolence.

37. Women's experience in life's realities of cleaning, feeding people, caring for babies, etc., makes their vision of reality clearer than men's.

44. Rape is best stopped by replacing the current male-oriented culture of violence with an alternative culture based on more gentle, womanly qualities.

50. Bringing more women into male-dominated professions would make the professions less cutthroat and competitive.

Women of Color Perspective:

3. In education and legislation to stop rape, ethnicity and race must be treated sensitively to ensure that women of color are protected equally.

8. Racism and sexism make double the oppression for women of color in the work environment.

12. Women of color have less legal and social service protection from being battered than White women have.

21. Women of color are oppressed by White standards of beauty.

26. Being put on a pedestal, which White women have protested, is a luxury that women of color have not had.

40. Antigay and racist prejudice act together to make it more difficult for gay male and lesbian people of color to maintain relationships.

43. In rape programs and workshops, not enough attention has been given to the special needs of women of color.

49. Discrimination in the workplace is worse for women of color than for all men and White women.

51. Much of the talk about power for women overlooks the need to empower people of all races and colors first.

(Continued)

Table 2.4   (continued)

57. The tradition of Afro-American women who are strong family leaders has strengthened the Afro-American community as a whole.

Fembehave Subscale:

Note: Items 61, 69, and 77, conceived as conservative behavior items, are not counted as part of the Fembehave scale . . . Items 64, 67, and 74 are reverse-scored.

61. My wedding was, or will be, celebrated with a full traditional ceremony.

62. I try to work only with groups in which there is shared leadership rather than hierarchies.

63. I actively try to integrate a communal form of work with a communal form of family life.

64. I have spoken against someone for overly affectionate behavior toward a member of the same sex in a public place.

65. I have participated in rape counseling because it was sensitive to issues of women of color.

66. I attend a place of worship that has changed the language of its prayer books and hymnals to reflect the equality of men and women.

67. My partner and I have followed the phases of the moon as a natural birth control method.

68. I have read nonexploitative erotica written from a woman's point of view.

69. I use the word "mankind" to refer to both men and women.

70. I use "she" rather than "he" generically, that is, to refer to an unknown person.

71. I take my child to a racially mixed child care center (or will when I have a child).

72. I try whenever I can to present an example of a nonviolent, noncompetitive alternative way of relating to people.

73. I often encourage women to take advantage of the many educational and legal opportunities available to them.

74. In my house we follow the religious rule that says that the wife should obey the husband.

75. I have participated in a protest against pornography.

76. I don't try to imitate or compete with the other sex either inside or outside the home.

77. All of my close family and friends are heterosexual.

78. I have participated in prochoice rallies (supporting freedom to have an abortion).

conferences (e.g., Ricketts, 1989), and a number of different gender-related beliefs (Martin et al., 2002). While this approach was found in all five journals analyzed, it was least typical in *PWQ*, somewhat regular in *G&S* and *W&P*, and common in *Signs* and the *NWSA Journal* (though the sample of articles in these two journals is admittedly very small).

Re-thinking Survey Research With Multiracial Feminism

Studies from each of these approaches have yielded important insights into contemporary feminism and gender issues more broadly. Individually, they have helped to clarify what it means to be a feminist, they have documented the complex relationship between feminist beliefs and identities, they have generated measurement tools to assess degrees and types of feminisms, and they have investigated how feminism impacts individuals' health and well-being.

Analyzing these studies from a multiracial feminist perspective, however, highlights important limitations of each general approach, particularly when used in the context of an isolated discipline. Researchers who use large-scale general–survey data generally benefit from diverse samples, but they are limited by simplistic measures of feminism. Within these studies, liberal feminism is centralized, and other varieties of feminism (and womanism) remain marginal and in many cases unacknowledged. Researchers who create their own survey instruments often employ more diverse and multidimensional measures of feminism, but tend to rely on a significantly less diverse pool of respondents. This approach to survey research, characteristic of psychological studies, relies heavily on samples of college students, the overwhelming majority of whom are white, economically privileged young adults. Researchers who employ particularistic survey research—the third approach described above—generally create their own survey instruments and often include diverse measures of feminism. While able to highlight the complexity of feminism, the emphasis on particularity within this approach limits researchers in their ability to draw meaningful comparisons across groups.

Secondary Data Analysis of General Surveys

The first general approach to survey research described above involves secondary data analysis of existing data. Within the sample of articles

I examined, slightly more than half of studies published in both *Women & Politics* and *Gender & Society* relied on secondary data analysis of national survey data, while studies in psychology or women's studies journals typically relied on smaller, local samples. This disciplinary difference in research *method* corresponds with an important difference in potential *measures*. Because survey researchers in psychology and women's and gender studies often design their own survey tools, sometimes adapting or combining the scales previously developed by others, their tool kit for measuring feminism is typically much larger. For example, as described above, Henley and colleagues (1998) use dozens of measures to understand feminism while studies relying on the ANES (and similar studies in sociology that rely on the General Social Survey) have only a handful of "feminist" measures at their disposal. With a limited number of feminist measures, it is very difficult to capture the diverse ways in which women (and men) approach feminism and gender issues more broadly. Instead, sociologists and political scientists typically rely on a few "good indicators" of feminism. From a multiracial feminist perspective, however, such measures are often problematic.

If we reconsider the measures used by Cook (1989), for example, we can see how multiracial feminism can inform—and arguably improve—this approach to survey research on feminism. As described above, Cook focuses on two dimensions of "politicized feminist consciousness" among women: individuals' beliefs about gender roles and a feeling thermometer of the women's movement. Her reliance on beliefs about gender roles centralizes one feminist perspective—liberal feminism—and does not do much to address other feminist perspectives. Cook argues that focusing on gender roles to measure feminism "makes good intuitive sense" as "anti-feminists will not believe that a woman should play an equal role with men in business and politics" (p. 77). While this assertion may be true, Cook's measure of feminism does not capture the core of socialist, radical, cultural, or multiracial feminist beliefs, all of which push for institutional and cultural change rather than equal opportunity.

Cook's (1989) reliance on women's feelings toward the women's movement as an indicator of their "feminist consciousness" is arguably more problematic. Recall that Cook analyzes data from 1972 to 1984, a time when multiracial feminist scholarship was flourishing. Recall too that much of the multiracial feminist scholarship at this time was highly critical of some aspects of the U.S. women's movement, on the grounds that it was exclusionary and in many ways reproducing, rather than challenging, social inequalities. We can imagine that an engaged, politicized multiracial feminist might have good reason to feel "cool" toward the women's movement. In fact, her cool feelings may be the product of her strong feminist consciousness.

If we examine these feminist measures without a multiracial feminist perspective, then they do seem to make sense intuitively. Indeed, we would expect that most feminists should feel more positive toward the women's movement, and we would further expect that most feminists would advocate equal opportunity in running business, government, and industry. But with a multiracial feminist perspective, we can see more clearly that the measures of feminism that Cook and others use represent a *particular kind* of feminism, and this particular kind of feminism has been historically associated with relatively privileged women.

If, in our survey research, we employ measures that are relatively reliable for one group but are significantly less reliable for another group, our findings are likely to be biased. More specifically, our research may suffer from *systematic measurement error,* which sociologists Singleton and Straits (1999, p. 115) describe as error that "results from factors that systematically influence either the process of measurement or the concept being measured." They provide an example of systematic measurement error by discussing cultural bias in IQ tests:

> Most IQ tests contain problems and language that tend to favor particular groups in society. Given the same "true" intelligence level, the person familiar with the test problems and language will always score higher than the person who is unfamiliar with the test problems or who speaks a different language than the one in which the test is communicated.

A similar phenomenon appears to be at work in much of feminist survey research. This research has relied on measures of feminism that, when analyzed from a multiracial feminist perspective, seem to privilege one feminist perspective over others—a perspective that is closely associated with a relatively privileged group of women.

Primary Data Analysis of Issue-Specific Surveys

Much of the survey research that has taken a more complex approach to measuring feminism suffers from a very different limitation: over-reliance on relatively homogenous samples. Though studies published in *PWQ* use a variety of measures and samples, my analysis reveals a relatively high reliance on college samples compared with other disciplines. Specifically, 19 of the 32 articles published in *PWQ* (59%) rely *entirely* on student samples (primarily undergraduates, though some involve graduate students), while only one sample article published outside of *PWQ* relies on data from a primarily student sample. Of the thirteen studies in *PWQ* that move beyond student samples, eight show use of samples primarily

from university or academic communities (such as alumnae or participants at academic conferences).

More than 25 years ago, psychologist Michelle Fine (1985) analyzed
the methodological approach of 106 articles published in *Psychology of
Women Quarterly* from 1978 to 1981, and she found that roughly half
relied on samples of college women. She concluded,

> The experiences of diverse groups of women, particularly those whose lives
> are neglected by prevailing ideologies and are absent from public view, need
> to gain further recognition in psychology of women. This literature currently
> mirrors traditional psychology with studies of white, middle-class, often pro-
> fessional women. (1985, p. 171)

My analysis of the 32 *PWQ* articles that investigate feminism shows a very
similar pattern. As mentioned above, more than half of the sample articles
published in *PWQ* use student-only samples. As a result, most of what we
know about feminism from these articles applies primarily to this particular
population—a population comprising mostly young adults, most of whom
are relatively privileged.

A multiracial feminist approach to survey research encourages us to
broaden our focus to include samples that are more diverse, not just with
respect to race and ethnicity but also with respect to age, class, sexuality, and nation. It encourages us to view respondents not just as isolated
individuals, but as people who are situated within particular social locations, people who occupy particular spaces within intersecting social
hierarchies.[x] Survey researchers are best able to do this when their samples
reflect the diversity of lived experiences, ideologies, and identities.

Primary Data Analysis of Particularistic Surveys

Much of the feminist survey research published in *NWSA Journal* and
Signs, and a small number of those articles published in the other three journals, also uses relatively homogenous samples. When doing so, however, they

---

[x] Michelle Fine (1992, p. 7) makes a similar point with regard to feminist psychology:
"Most feminist psychologists have yet to declare questions of power primary; to
establish white, heterosexual, patriarchal control as central to relations and
representations of gender; and to take seriously the spaces that women create as
retreats, celebrations, as moments of resistance, and as the closets for our social
transformations. . . . In our attempts to bring feminism to psychology, we have
perhaps undermined the politics and scholarship of feminism, refused questions of
power and asymmetry, and defaulted to the benign study of gender differences."

emphasize the particularity of their research and their findings. Runyan and Wenning (2004), for example, study feminist activism in one specific geographic location (Montgomery County, Ohio); Carbert (1994) studies feminism among farm women in Ontario; and Martin, Reynolds, and Keith (2002) investigate feminist consciousness among Florida attorneys and judges. In each case, the authors consider the broad implications of their findings but are careful to situate these findings within the particulars of their research projects. In contrast to the other approaches discussed, these studies are less geared toward creating broadly applicable measures or documenting universalistic relationships. Rather, they use survey research to present in-depth case studies rooted in the particular.

Studies that investigate feminism as it relates to one particular group, and that employ measures of feminism that are designed specifically for that group (as in the third approach above), are potentially in the best position to capture the complexity of feminism. As is the case with ethnographic studies of feminism, however this approach is limited. By studying one specific group, scholars lose the ability to make direct comparisons of this group's experiences with those of others. As McCall (2005, p. 1773) explains in her article "The Complexity of Intersectionality," by using an *intercategorical* approach, scholars can "provisionally adopt existing analytic categories to document relationships of inequality among social groups and changing configurations of inequality along multiple and conflicting dimensions." But if in our survey research we focus exclusively on one social group, then intercategorical complexity is lost and so is our ability to understand how the experiences and identities of individuals within our sample relate to, and are shaped by, the experiences of those outside of it.

In their essay "Theorizing Difference From Multiracial Feminism," Baca Zinn and Thornton Dill explain that multiracial feminism "focuses not just on differences, but also on the way in which differences and domination intersect and are historically and socially constituted" (1996, p. 329). Historian Elsa Barkley Brown makes a similar point in her essay "What Has Happened Here? The Politics of Difference in Women's History and Feminist Politics." Barkley Brown (1992, p. 298) writes that "recognizing and even including difference is, in and of itself, not enough."

> Rather, "We need to recognize not only differences but also the relational nature of those differences. Middle-class white women's lives are not just different from working-class white, Black, and Latina women's lives. It is important to recognize that middle-class women live the lives they do precisely because working-class women live the lives they do. White women and women of color not only live different lives but white women live the lives they do in large part because women of color live the ones they do."

While survey research rooted in the particular is well positioned to capture the complexity of feminism in women's (and men's) lives, it is simultaneously limited in its ability to capture the relational bases of this complexity.

Survey research on specific varieties of feminism within a specific community and within a specific context can produce a complex and nuanced narrative of feminism. Yet at the same time, this kind of research is perhaps at the greatest risk of perpetuating "patchwork quilt" (Baca Zinn et al.) or "mosaic" models (May, 2010) of difference. *Differences* are highlighted in these approaches, but the processes through which differences are created are obscured. We may gain new understandings of feminism among, for instance, Ontario farm women or women in Ohio, but we are left to guess how these groups relate to one another.

The Compounding Effects of Disciplinarity

Each of the three approaches described above brings a unique combination of benefits and limitations to the analysis of feminism. Studies of feminism in which researchers use national survey data benefit from diverse samples, but are simultaneously limited in their measures of feminism. Psychological studies of feminism, in contrast, rely on more nuanced and multidimensional measures of feminism, but are limited by their overreliance on homogenous, relatively privileged samples. Particularistic studies of feminism tend to rely on homogenous samples and of nuanced measures of feminism designed for a specific population. It is precisely this particularity, however, that makes it difficult for researchers to draw comparisons across groups and to understand the meaning of difference.

It is, of course, impossible for one study to capture all of the complexity of feminism as it relates to diverse social groups. And specialization in and of itself is not necessarily incompatible with multiracial feminist research. When any one disciplinary approach is used in isolation from others, however, we are less likely to recognize "the blind spots and structures of exclusion" that are embedded in our analyses. One of the key benefits of interdisciplinary research is that it allows scholars the opportunity to critically examine research practices and knowledge claims that are often taken for granted. It positions scholars to situate their own research within a broader and more complex intellectual field.

While feminist scholars largely agree on the merits of interdisciplinarity, the analyses in this chapter reveal that disciplinary divisions continue to structure feminist dialogue and that scholars in different disciplines tend to approach survey research in different ways. We saw in Figure 2.1, for example, that survey researchers in psychology turn again and again to Henley's

(1998) analysis of feminism (article 22 in Figure 2.1), while researchers in political science are more likely to cite Cook's 1989 work (article 50) and researchers in sociology the work of Rhodebeck (1996) and Hunter and Sellers (1998), (articles 38 and 37, respectively). Rather than seeing feminist scholars situate their research within an interdisciplinary field, we see them situating their work primarily within the bounds of a particular discipline. Rather than finding scholars reach across methodological divides, to complicate and contextualize, we see the reinscribing of disciplinary limitations. The limitations associated with simplistic measures are compounded within political science and sociology, and the limitations of homogenous samples are compounded within psychology. As a group, the five articles published in *Signs* and *NWSA Journal* do not fall into this pattern, but the fact that none is cited by any of the articles in the sample suggests that these journals remain on the margins of feminist survey research.

Conclusion

In her essay "(Inter)disciplinarity and the Question of the Women's Studies Ph.D.," Susan Stanford Friedman argues that feminist scholars across disciplinary divisions "may well share a certain core of feminist theory that shapes some of their research questions, but they hardly share a common methodological language and can barely understand each other's research" (1998, p. 315). In the case of survey research, feminist scholars *do* share a common methodological language (though their accents may differ) and, in general, *can* understand each other's research. And yet as we have seen here, disciplinary divisions remain strong.

In her book *Meeting the Universe Halfway*, feminist physicist Karen Barad (2007, p. 93) writes that "[w]hat is needed are respectful engagements with different disciplinary practices, not course-grained portrayals that make caricatures of another discipline from some position outside it." In bringing a multiracial feminist critique to contemporary feminist survey research, I have tried to meet this standard. On the one hand, each of the above approaches has made significant contributions to feminist scholarship, as well as to the social sciences. On the other hand, a multiracial feminist critique of these disciplinary approaches reveals important limitations—especially when produced within the context of an isolated discipline.

Given this situation, how can we foster respectful engagements between multiracial feminism on the one hand and disciplinary methodological practices on the other? How might bridging multiracial feminism with survey research help us to identify the "cultural elements" that shape scientific inquiry and to "figure out which of these cultural elements are at this particular historical moment advancing and which blocking the growth of knowledge" (Harding, 1998, p. 145)? How might survey research rooted in multiracial feminism help us to disrupt the universalistic representations of social phenomena that are often presented in large-scale survey research? What does multiracial feminist, post-positivist survey research even look like?

These are the questions I address in the next four chapters. I argue that a multiracial feminist, post-positivist approach to survey research goes beyond simply "fixing" each of the three disciplinary approaches described above. Such an approach requires transforming and reappropriating survey research techniques. It requires combining the insights from each of the approaches described above and combining them with contributions from the humanities. Identifying the cultural elements at work within socio-logical survey research is difficult if we remain strictly within the realm of sociological theory and methods. The same holds true for psychological, political, or gender studies research. Often it is only when we consider an alternative approach that we are able to see how our theoretical and meth-odological frameworks have limited the possibilities for discovery.

In the next three chapters, I explore what it might mean to bring a mul-tiracial feminist framework to social science survey research. Chapter 3, which focuses on sexism, shows how a multiracial feminist approach can inform analyses of large-scale general surveys. Chapter 4, which focuses on racial and ethnic discrimination, shows how a multiracial feminist approach can inform studies that use multi-item scales. Chapter 5, which focuses on feminist identities and *gender-conscious* identities more broadly, shows how a multiracial feminist framework can inform particularistic survey research. Each chapter presents a different approach to multiracial feminist survey research, and there are undoubtedly more approaches than those I present here. As I show in the next three chapters, a multiracial feminist approach to survey research is important for the social sciences not only because it highlights difference and inequality, but also because it can improve the quality of our models. In other words, it is vital not only for a feminist agenda, but also for those interested in doing quality survey research.

3

Analytic Interventions of Multiracial Feminism

Measuring and Modeling Sexism With an Intersectional Approach

"[C]ategories of discrimination may overlap, and ... individuals may suffer historical exclusion on the basis of both race and gender, age and physical handicap, or some other combination. The situation of individuals who confront multiple grounds of disadvantage is particularly complex. Categorizing such discrimination as primarily racially oriented, or primarily gender-oriented, misconceives the reality of discrimination as it is experienced by individuals."

~Madam Justice L'Heureux-Dubé (1993; qtd. in Ontario Human Rights Commission, 2001, p. 5)

Introduction

In the previous chapter, I argued that, despite feminist theorists' commitment to interdisciplinary scholarship, disciplinary boundaries remain very significant in survey research on feminism. Disciplinary norms influence the *kinds* of questions that researchers ask, as well as the theoretical perspectives used to *frame* these questions. In addition, disciplinary traditions influence how scholars answer the questions they pose: the kinds of *data* that are collected and the *techniques* employed to analyze these data. Disciplinary boundaries also work to shape feminist dialogues. Though they may share scholarly interests and political commitments, many feminist scholars remain locked in dialogue with those scholars who share similar academic backgrounds: psychologists with psychologists, sociologists with sociologists, political scientists with political scientists, social scientists with social scientists. There are exceptions to this, of course, but overall disciplinary boundaries remain an integral part of feminist survey research. While each disciplinary approach to social science survey research has limitations, each approach has also yielded significant contributions to scholarly debates and, just as important, to "real world" feminist issues.

In this chapter, I explore the implications of multiracial feminism for survey research on sexism and gender discrimination. Survey research on sexism, like that on feminism, can be grouped into three broad categories: studies that employ large-scale, general surveys; studies that use medium-scale but more focused surveys (often including multi-item scales); and small-scale studies designed to assess sexism as experienced by particular groups. And, just as a multiracial feminist perspective can illuminate the benefits and limitations associated with each approach for measuring and modeling feminism, a multiracial feminist perspective can also shed light on the benefits and limitations of each approach for understanding and analyzing sexism and gender discrimination.

I begin this chapter by reviewing some of the most commonly used measures of sexism in the social sciences. My aim is not to denigrate previous work on sexism but rather to use this work as a springboard, from which researchers might develop a multiracial feminist approach to survey research on gender discrimination. After reviewing the measures of gender discrimination, I turn my attention to issues of statistical modeling. How might a statistical analysis that uses multiracial feminist theory as its starting point look? There are many ways of combining the insights of multiracial feminism with survey research; in this chapter, I use data from the General Social Survey (GSS) to demonstrate one approach.

Situating Gender Discrimnation and Harassment Within a Multiracial Feminist Framework

More than thirty years ago, three members of the Combahee River Collective, Barbara Smith, Beverly Smith, and Demita Frazier, wrote a

"A Black Feminist Statement" in which they described the origins and continued need for black feminism. They wrote:

> The most general statement of our politics at the present time would be that we are actively committed to struggling against racial, sexual, heterosexual, and class oppression and see as our particular task *the development of integrated analysis and practice based upon the fact that the major systems of oppression are interlocking.* The synthesis of these oppressions creates the conditions of our lives. (1981 [The statement was originally dated April 1977], p. 210, italics added for emphasis)

The Collective's description of "interlocking" systems of oppression provided the foundation for intersectional theories that developed over the next three decades. As explained in Chapter 1, theories of intersectionality understand gender as a system of inequality that is deeply connected to—and even shaped by—other systems of inequality. As suggested in "A Black Feminist Statement," individuals do not experience gender in isolation from race, class, and sexuality. Nor do individuals experience gender separately from age, disability status, or nation. Rather, social statuses are *lived simultaneously,* which means that one's experiences "as a woman" are simultaneously shaped by one's racial status, class position, and age, as well as by other social statuses. As Baca Zinn, Hondagneu-Sotelo, and Messner (2007, p. 153) write, "[n]obody experiences themselves as solely gendered. Instead, gender is configured through cross-cutting forms of difference that carry deep social and economic consequences."

The notion of simultaneity carries several important implications for understanding and analyzing sexism and gender discrimination. The first concerns the particular forms of discrimination that individuals encounter. Multiracial feminist theories posit that gendered stereotypes and sexist practices are oftentimes based not only on gender but also on multiple intersecting social statuses. In so far as discriminatory practices are based on racialized, classed, sexualized, and age-specific gender stereotypes, the particular form of sexism that an individual encounters is, in part, shaped by her location within these intersecting hierarchies. As Baca Zinn and Thornton Dill write (1996, pp. 326–327), "people experience race, class, gender, and sexuality differently depending upon their social location in the structures of race, class, gender, and sexuality." In other words, while there may be similarities among different groups of women, women of different racial groups tend to experience different kinds of gender discrimination (see, for example, Buchanan, Settles, & Woods, 2008). The same holds true for women of diverse socioeconomic statuses and different age groups.

A second insight of multiracial feminism concerns the social-spatial contexts in which individuals experience gender discrimination. Writing primarily about racial discrimination, sociologist Joe Feagin (1991, p. 102) argued that "there is a spatial dimension to discrimination" and that the probability of encountering racial discrimination depends in part on the environment one is in (see also Feagin & Eckberg, 1980; Roscigno, 2007). A multiracial feminist approach takes this idea one step further, emphasizing that the particular spaces that one moves through on a day-to-day basis are largely determined by intersecting hierarchies of race, gender, class, and age.[i]

Though it may seem obvious, it is nonetheless important to note that social-spatial contexts shape both the likelihood that women will face gender discrimination as well as the particular form of discrimination that women ultimately face. Moreover, the contexts that women move through are shaped not only by their gender status but by other social statuses as well: age, race, class, nation, and sexuality. To be the target of gender discrimination in promotion, for example, one must be working in the paid labor force. Working-class women, whose jobs often lack opportunities for advancement, may be less likely than upper-class women to experience gender discrimination in promotion, simply because so few promotion opportunities actually exist in "dead-end" jobs. Women's experiences with sexual harassment are similarly shaped by social-spatial contexts. Women working in occupations held predominately by women, particularly when their supervisors are also women, are less likely to be tokenized and thus are less likely to be the target of overt sexual harassment. In contrast, women who are disempowered relative to their male coworkers may be targeted more often (Chamberlain, Crowley, Tope, & Hodson, 2008; Fitzgerald, 1993; Kanter, 1977/1993; Kohlman, 2006; Pierce, 2010). Women's structural location in the labor force influences the type of sexism that women encounter and their structural location in the labor force is linked to a number of other factors. From a multiracial feminist perspective, it is important to consider how social statuses other than gender interact with gender to shape the different social-spatial contexts in which women face discrimination and harassment.

Multiracial feminist theorists' focus on simultaneity offers a third insight into gender discrimination—one that is particularly important for those who are trying to measure gender discrimination, as opposed to discrimination based on age, race, class, or sexuality. In short, because social statuses are experienced simultaneously, it is sometimes difficult

---

[i] Here I am building on an argument that Mosi Ifatunji and I made concerning the importance of context for understanding racial discrimination (see Harnois & Ifatunji, 2011).

for individuals to discern whether their experiences of mistreatment result from one particular status or another. As suggested in the opening quotation to this chapter, discriminatory practices are oftentimes based on multiple social statuses, and encouraging individuals to identify one (and only one) particular "cause" for their mistreatment may be inappropriate. Legal scholar Kimberle Crenshaw (1991, p. 1244) writes,

> [M]any of the experiences Black women face are not subsumed within the traditional boundaries of race or gender discrimination as these boundaries are currently understood. . . . [T]he intersection of racism and sexism factors into Black women's lives in ways that cannot be captured wholly by looking at the race or gender dimensions of those experiences separately.

In other words, because social statuses are experienced simultaneously, it is often difficult to determine whether one's experiences result from one particular status or another. This is particularly important when individuals occupy more than one underprivileged position. Imagine a hardworking middle-aged woman who occupies privileged positions on hierarchies of class, able-bodiedness, sexuality, race, and ethnicity. When this particular woman realizes she has been treated unfairly—let's say she has been denied a promotion in her job despite being the most qualified—she may attribute this mistreatment to her being a woman. "Clearly a sexist act!" she may conclude. But now imagine another woman, a young African American woman, who experiences the same event. She too realizes that she has been treated unfairly but wonders, "Is this because of my gender? Or my race? Or my age? Or maybe all three?" It may be that this second act, too, is mostly—or even entirely—about sexism. It is equally likely— perhaps even more so—that this discrimination was based on race, age, or some combination of the three. The point is that for people who occupy multiple marginalized statuses, the answer is oftentimes not clear-cut. Survey research that asks individuals to attribute their mistreatment to a particular social status may be forcing an inappropriate frame on the respondents' experiences.

Taken as a whole, multiracial feminist theory urges researchers to consider how social statuses other than gender intersect with gender to shape women's experiences with sexism and discrimination. It is important to note that this approach stops short of making absolute, universal claims about the particulars of intersectionality, as some social statuses may be more important than others in particular contexts. As Patricia Hill Collins (2000, p. 228) writes, "regardless of how any given matrix [of oppression] is actually organized either across time or from society to society, the concept of a matrix of domination encapsulates the universality of intersecting oppressions as organized through diverse local realities." From a theoretical and methodological perspective, it is important to consider the *possibility* of these intersections (Yuval-Davis, 2006). For, as will become clear in the next section, if these intersections are not considered explicitly, they are often either obscured or erased entirely.

Measuring Gender Discrimination and Harassment

To demonstrate the importance of a multiracial approach for understanding and researching sexism, I briefly review three measures of sexism from the social sciences. I first consider Klonoff and Landrine's (1995) Schedule of Sexist Events (SSE), which is among the most comprehensive and widely used scales of sexism in psychology. I then examine the General Social Survey's (GSS's) questions concerning interpersonal discrimination at work. The General Social Survey is one of the most commonly used surveys in American sociology; it contains only a handful of questions pertaining to discrimination, but the survey is administered biennially to a large, diverse sample. Finally, I compare these more general measures with those employed in a more particular survey: the American Association of University Women's (AAUW's) Drawing the Line: Sexual Harassment on Campus (Hill & Silva, 2005).

The Schedule of Sexist Events

One of the best measures of gender discrimination, one of the most comprehensive and widely used in contemporary psychology, is Klonoff and Landrine's (1995) Schedule of Sexist Events (SSE), which is presented in Table 3.1. Klonoff and Landrine developed the SSE in part because they realized the importance of sexism in the everyday lives of women, and they wanted a way to measure empirically the negative impact of sexism on the physical and mental health of women (1995, p. 440). Their measure of interpersonal sexism includes 20 event-specific items, encompassing sexist degradation (such as being called a sexist name), sexist discrimination in distant relationships (for example, being treated unfairly by people in service jobs), sexism in close relationships (for example, being treated unfairly by a boyfriend or husband), and sexist discrimination in the workplace (such as being denied a raise, promotion, or tenure or another such thing at work). Klonoff and Landrine "conceptualize the various domains/types of [gender] discrimination as 'sexist events,'" viewing them, in their words, "as gender-specific stressors . . . that happen *to women, because they are women*" (1995, p. 441, italics in original). When they introduced the SSE, Klonoff and Landrine presented substantial evidence to document the

Table 3.1   Questions From the Schedule of Sexist Events Survey.

1. How many times have you been treated unfairly by teachers or professors because you are a woman?

2. How many times have you been treated unfairly by your employer, boss or supervisors because you are a woman?

3. How many times have you been treated unfairly by your co-workers, fellow students or colleagues because you are a woman?

4. How many times have you been treated unfairly by people in service jobs (by store clerks, waiters, bartenders, waitresses, bank tellers, mechanics and others) because you are a woman?

5. How many times have you been treated unfairly by strangers because you are a woman?

6. How many times have you been treated unfairly by people in helping jobs (by doctors, nurses, psychiatrists, case workers, dentists, school counselors, therapists, pediatricians, school principals, gynecologists, and others) because you are a woman?

7. How many times have you been treated unfairly by neighbors because you are a woman?

9. How many times have you been treated unfairly by your boyfriend, husband, or other important man in your life because you are a woman?

10. How many times were you denied a raise, a promotion, tenure, a good assignment, a job, or other such thing at work that you deserved because you are a woman?

11. How many times have you been treated unfairly by your family because you are a woman?

13. How many times have people made inappropriate or unwanted sexual advances to you because you are a woman?

14. How many times have people failed to show you the respect that you deserve because you are a woman?

15. How many times have you wanted to tell someone off for being sexist?

16. How many times have you been really angry about something sexist that was done to you?

17. How many times were you forced to take drastic steps (such as filing a grievance, filing a lawsuit, quitting your job, moving away, and other actions) to deal with some sexist thing that was done to you?

18. How many times have you been called a sexist name like bitch, cunt, chick or other names?

19. How many times have you gotten into an argument or a fight about something sexist that was done or said to you or done to somebody else?

20. How many times have you been made fun of, picked on, pushed, shoved, hit, or threatened with harm because you are a woman?

(continued)

Table 3.1   (continued)

21. How many times have you heard people making sexist jokes, or degrading sexual jokes?

23. How different would your life be now if you HAD NOT BEEN treated in a sexist and unfair way?

Note: Because items 8, 12, and 22 did not load on any factor, they were omitted from the SSE and are not shown (qtd. from table in Klonoff & Landrine, 1995).
Source: Klonoff and Landrine, 1995.

scale's reliability and validity.[ii] They conducted factor analyses of the scale for lifetime and recent (within the past year) sexist events; they tested the structure of the scale for various groups of women, including women of different ages, ethnic groups, and marital statuses, and they analyzed the relationship between the SSE and two other measures of stressful events, the Hassles Frequency and the PERI-Life Events scales.

Since its creation, the Schedule of Sexist Events scale has been used in a variety of psychological studies, both to document the pervasiveness of sexism and to assess the negative consequences that arise from sexist events.[iii] It is a widely used measure for good reason: There is much to like about this scale. Unlike general measures of sexist discrimination, the survey items in the SSE remind women to think about specific kinds of sexist discrimination. One of its questions (Q18), for example, asks women, "How many times have you been called a sexist name like bitch, cunt, chick or other names?" The question itself may serve as a reminder to those women who don't think regularly about sexist language, that these names are deeply gendered and problematic. Likewise, another question (Q21) asks, "How many times have you heard people making sexist jokes or degrading sexual jokes?" For some women, the question in and of itself may serve as a reminder that sexist jokes, though unfortunately ubiquitous, are an example of sexist behavior. Because of these built-in reminders of what sexism entails, women's responses to these survey questions may provide more accurate information

---

[ii] "Reliability" refers to the "stability or consistency of an operational definition" and "validity" refers to the "congruence or 'goodness of fit' between an operational definition and the concept it is supposed to measure" (Singleton & Straits, 1999, pp. 565, 570).

[iii] For example, Landrine, Klonoff, Gibbs, Manning, and Lund (1995) used the SSE to investigate the impact of sexism on women's psychiatric and physical well-being, Sabik and Tylka (2006) used the SSE to examine how feminism mediates the relationship between perceived sexist events and disordered eating, and Yoder and McDonald (1998) used a subscale of the SSE to document sexism aimed at women firefighters.

than general questions about sexism (e.g., "Have you experienced sexism within the past year?"). In addition to prodding for specific sexist events, another merit of the SSE is that it asks women about many different types of sexist events and events that occur in a wide range of interpersonal relationships. For example, it asks respondents about their experiences in work and school settings, in addition to their experiences in their family life and in their public life (e.g., "How many times have you been treated unfairly by strangers because you are a woman?" [Q5]). Finally, the SSE is an important tool for documenting sexism because it asks women not only *whether* they have ever experienced a particular sexist event, but also it asks whether they have experienced a particular event recently (i.e., within the past year) and how frequently each event happened.[iv] As a result, the SSE allows researchers to compare how women respond to isolated incidents of sexism as compared to how they respond to repeated sexist events.

Though the merits of the SSE are numerous, a multiracial feminist analysis of the SSE reveals some important limitations. The first concerns the differing contexts in which people experience discrimination and the ways in which these contexts intersect with differing social statuses. The SSE asks questions concerning respondents' experiences in school (e.g., Q1, Q3), at work (e.g., Q3, Q2, Q10, Q17), in their home lives (e.g., Q7, Q9, Q11), and in public places (e.g., Q4, Q6). While it is important for surveys to tap a wide range of contexts, doing so generates a potential problem. Because some groups move through particular contexts more than others, questions that focus on experiences within these contexts (e.g., work experiences) will tap the experiences of some groups more than others. These kinds of questions will give more weight to some groups' experiences with discrimination than to others' and thus introduce potential bias in the measurement tool.

Consider, for example, the SSE-Recent scale, which asks respondents about their experiences with sexism in the past year. Q10 asks, "How many times were you denied a raise, a promotion, tenure, a good assignment, a job, or other such thing at work that you deserved because you are a woman?" Q17 asks, "How many times were you forced to take drastic steps (such as filing a grievance, filing a lawsuit, quitting your job, moving away and other actions) to deal with some sexist thing that was done to you?" Women who are retired, women who have not yet entered the workforce, and other women who are not currently working would probably indicate that the event has "never happened to you" in the past year.

[iv] Respondents are asked for lifetime and recent sexist events whether the event occurred "never, once in a while, sometimes, a lot, most of the time, or almost all of the time."

Women working in low-wage jobs without opportunities for promotion and with few employment opportunities elsewhere may also score low on these questions. (If there are no raises or promotions to be had, one can't be denied in the first place; if there are limited options for employment elsewhere, one may be less likely to respond to sexist events with "drastic" measures.) These women's low score on this variable would then be added to their scores on the other 19 survey items, giving them a total score for recent gender discrimination. While tallying women's experiences in this way can certainly yield important insights, this approach is limited in that the resulting totals (e.g., a total score of 40, 65, or 100) mask the differences in women's opportunities to experience particular types of sexism. As Matteson and Moradi (2005, pp. 53–54) have noted, reliance on total scores of the SSE "might blur important distinctions in specific dimensions of sexist events [e.g., sexist events at work or school vs. sexist events in intimate relationships] when specific outcome variables are considered."

There is, of course, good reason to ask women about their experiences with sexism in a variety of settings. Doing so allows researchers to determine the contexts in which women experience sexism most frequently and can help to determine if sexist events in some contexts are more damaging than those in others. Moreover, because women do experience different kinds of sexism in different settings (being denied a raise at work is a very different experience from being treated unfairly by your family because you are a woman), it is important for researchers who are seeking to assess the prevalence of sexism, to ask women about their experiences in a number of different contexts. From a multiracial feminist perspective, however, a measure that includes questions that tap for sexist events in some contexts and not others is a *potential* source of bias. As mentioned above, the SSE asks questions concerning respondents' experiences in school, at work, in their home lives, and in public places. It does not ask about sexist experiences within religious institutions, it does not ask women about sexist images they have encountered in media, and, increasingly important, it does not ask women about their experience with virtual sexism—sexist events on Facebook, Internet chat rooms, over e-mail, and the like (how many of us who regularly use computers have not encountered sexist images online?). Again, the (potential) problem is not that the SSE does not speak to every social-spatial context in which sexism can possibly occur. But rather, when some social-spatial contexts are over-represented and others are under-represented and when the differing representation correlates with differences in social statuses (e.g., age, racial, class-based statuses), then the measurement tool is potentially biased. It may measure some groups' experiences better than other groups', and if this is the case, then the conclusions we draw across groups can be particularly misleading.

A second potential source of bias concerns the particular types of sexism that individuals may encounter in any given context. A multiracial feminist perspective highlights how social statuses other than gender (e.g., age, class and power, race and ethnicity) influence the particular types of sexism that women encounter (Baca Zinn et al., 2007; Crenshaw, 1991; Crenshaw, 1992; Welsh, Carr, MacQuarrie, & Huntley, 2006). And while the SSE does include questions that cover a wide range of sexist events, none of the questions explicitly tap for sexist events as they intersect with racism, ageism, or homophobia. For example, Q18 asks, "How many times have you been called a sexist name like bitch, cunt, chick or other names?" The question stops short, though, of including racialized, homophobic, and ageist sexist terms, such as "girl," "dyke," or "baby mama." While these racist-sexist, ageist-sexist, and homophobic-sexist "hybrids" are likely not applied to all—or even most—women, it is also likely that some women experience hybrid forms of discrimination more frequently than they experience "pure" sexism. And this may be particularly true for women who occupy more than one marginal status. In addition to assessing the particular forms of sexism that *are* included in the SSE, then, a multiracial feminist perspective encourages us to think through what types of sexism are *not* included. It may be that women who experience racist-sexist, ageist-sexist, or homophobic-sexist hybrids understand this mistreatment to be a result of their status as a woman, and if this is true, then perhaps these events are indeed represented within the Schedule of Sexist Events survey. However, a multiracial feminist perspective pushes us to consider how the exclusion of specific racialized sexist events and other hybrid types of discrimination may affect researchers' findings and conclusions.

A third, related limitation of the SSE concerns the lack of attention paid to other types of discrimination and the way in which respondents are asked to classify their mistreatment. On the majority of the survey items (13 of 20), respondents are asked if their mistreatment was due to their status as a woman (for example, Q2 asks, "How many times have you been treated unfairly by your employer, boss or supervisors because you are a woman?"). In fact, this "single-oppression framework" is built into Klonoff and Landrine's definition of a "sexist event": "Sexist events . . . are negative events (stressors) that happen *to women, because they are women*" (1995, p. 441). As mentioned above, many multiracial feminist scholars have argued that, for people with multiple minority statuses, it is often difficult, if not impossible, to attribute discriminatory acts to one (and only one) social status. This is because discriminatory acts are often based on multiple intersecting statuses. For example, when asked about her experiences with sexual harassment, one Filipino live-in caregiver in Welsh et al.'s study explained, "It's like a mix. It's a mix action. You don't know if it is if that person is doing it to you because of the color of your skin and the type of job that you have, you're doing the dirty job in the house so you don't know if it is harassment or sexual harassment" (2006, p. 96). A recent review of complaints filed with the Ontario Human Rights Commission underscores the importance of intersectionality for understanding discrimination and harassment. Of the complaints filed between April 1997 and December 2000, almost half—48%—cited more than one ground of discrimination (Ontario Human Rights Commission, 2001, p. 11).

It is of course necessary when studying gender discrimination or sexism to ask respondents what they feel the basis of their mistreatment was. And it is, of course, important to distinguish between those incidents of discrimination based primarily on gender and those based primarily on race, ethnicity, sexual orientation, or age. However, it is equally important to consider the potential bias that is introduced when asking women to determine the primary cause of their mistreatment. Women with only one marginal status—that is, women who are privileged with respect to age, race, ethnicity, able-bodiedness, and sexual orientation—are perhaps more likely to attribute their mistreatment to their gender status ("I have been mistreated 'because I am a woman.'"). Women with multiple marginalized statuses may be less likely to attribute their mistreatment to their status "as a woman"—even if they experience a "sexist event." Instead, women may attribute their mistreatment to their status "as a young woman" or "as a lesbian woman" or "a black woman" (see, for example, Buchanan & Omerod, 2002; Cortina, 2001; Welsh et al., 2006). In short, a multiracial feminist perspective encourages us to examine the broader context of inequality in which discriminatory acts are experienced. It encourages researchers to view sexism as occurring alongside and in combination with other forms of discrimination and harassment.

The General Social Survey

In sharp contrast to the multi-item Schedule of Sexist Events scale, survey researchers in sociology have generally used single-item measures of sexism and gender discrimination, such as those found in the General Social Survey. The GSS, a source commonly used in sociological research, asks a range of questions concerning individuals' attitudes, experiences, and behaviors, as well as a number of questions concerning the respondents' backgrounds (e.g., family income, parents' educational attainment, when the respondent had her or his first child). The GSS has been conducted on a biennial basis in the United States, beginning in 1972. The data for each year represent an independent sample of English-speaking and, in the 2006 through 2010 samples, English- or Spanish-speaking persons 18 years of age or over who are not living in institutions (e.g., prisons or mental health facilities). In the 2002 and 2006 versions of the GSS, the questionnaire included a special series of questions concerning respondents' quality of working life. Included in this section were five questions concerning discrimination and harassment in the workplace:

Do you feel in any way discriminated against on your job because of your age?

Do you feel in any way discriminated against on your job because of your gender?

Do you feel in any way discriminated against on your job because of your race or ethnic origin?

In the last 12 months, were you sexually harassed by anyone while you were on the job?

In the last 12 months, were you threatened or harassed in any other way by anyone while you were on the job?

Compared to the numerous and more nuanced Schedule of Sexist Events questions, the GSS's questions on discrimination seem quite meager. The GSS asks only two questions concerning interpersonal sexism, and unlike in the SSE, where respondents report both how often sexist events occurred and how recently, in the GSS, respondents' answers are simply coded "yes," "no," or "I don't know." Whereas the SSE questions remind respondents about the multiple forms of sexism and gender discrimination, the GSS questions do not. Whereas the SSE asks questions about sexist experiences in a variety of contexts, the GSS does not. Though the survey has, over the years, included a number of questions concerning gender-related attitudes and has been used to assess gender-related prejudices and gender inequality more broadly, it is clearly limited in its ability to assess women's experiences with interpersonal sexism.

When analyzed from a multiracial feminist perspective, the GSS questions concerning discrimination share many of the same limitations as the SSE. The GSS questions assess women's experience in only one context— their place of work—and hence cannot be used to understand sexism experienced by women who are not working. Nor are these questions useful for understanding sexism directed at women workers outside of their place of employment (e.g., in schools or in public spaces). As was the case with the SSE, the discrimination and harassment questions in the GSS do not explicitly tap for sexist events as they intersect with racism, ageism, or homophobia. Finally, though the relative generality of the GSS questions might give respondents more room to interpret their experiences with discrimination and harassment, the GSS questions, like those in the SSE, encourage respondents to view systems of inequality, and the discrimination that results, as distinct. In other words, the survey instrument implies that people experience discrimination based on a single characteristic—gender, or race, or ethnicity, or age.

Despite these limitations, the GSS measures of workplace discrimination have two clear advantages relative to the SSE. First, because the survey is designed to capture diverse forms of workplace discrimination, the GSS includes questions about not only gender discrimination and sexual harassment but also racism, ageism, and "other" types of harassment. In this way, it is possible to analyze women's experiences with sexism as they intersect with other systems of inequality. Second, because the GSS is a national survey, analyses using the GSS are more generalizable to the overall U.S. population. The diversity of respondents included in the GSS allows researchers to highlight what McCall (2005, p. 1773) calls "inter-categorical complexity"—the "relationships of inequality among social groups and changing configurations of inequality along multiple and conflicting dimensions."

AAUW: Drawing the Line

In contrast to the SSE and the GSS survey instruments, the American Association of University Women (AAUW) recently conducted a survey designed to examine sexual harassment as experienced by one particular group: "U.S. residents ages 18 to 24 who were enrolled in college between January and May 2005" (Hill & Silva, 2005, p. 42). Like the questions in the GSS, those in the AAUW's Drawing the Line survey aimed to assess sexism as it occurs within one particular context, American colleges and universities. Researchers asked men and women both about the prevalence of sexual harassment on their school campus, as well as whether and how frequently they themselves had experienced particular types of sexual harassment. Table 3.2 lists the questions concerning respondents' own experiences of sexual harassment.

When compared to the GSS and SSE, what is perhaps most noticeable about the Drawing the Line survey is the specificity of questions concerning sexual harassment. While the SSE and the GSS contained questions concerning sexual harassment, in these survey instruments sexual harassment was included as one among many types of discrimination (as in the case of the GSS) or sexism (as in the case of the SSE). Since the Drawing the Line survey focuses only on sexual harassment—and only on sexual harassment as experienced by students on American college and university campuses, it is able to be much more specific. Through it, researchers ask questions

Table 3.2   Selected Questions From AAUW's Drawing the Line Survey.

Types of Sexual Harassment: *"During your whole college life, how often, if at all, has anyone (this includes students, teachers, other school employees, or anyone else) done the following things to you when you did not want them to?"*	Social-Spatial Contexts: *"Thinking about the types of sexual harassment in the previous question that you have experienced during your college life, have you ever been harassed . . . ?"*	Perpetrators: *Thinking about the types of sexual harassment in the previous question you have experienced during your college life, have you ever been harassed by . . . ? Please select all that apply.*
1. Made sexual comments, jokes, gestures, or looks	1. In a classroom, lecture hall (or laboratory)	1. A student
2. Showed, gave or left me sexual pictures, photographs, webpages, illustrations, messages or notes	2. In the hall, lounge or common area of a campus building	2. A former student
3. Posted sexual messages about me on the Internet (e.g., websites, blogs) or e-mailed, instant messaged or text messaged sexual messages about me	3. In the athletic facility, gym, playing field or pool area	3. A professor
4. Spread sexual rumors about me	4. In a locker room or restroom (other than in a dorm or student housing)	4. A teaching assistant
5. Called me gay or a lesbian or a homophobic name (such as faggot, dyke or queer)	5. In the cafeteria or meal hall	5. A counselor
6. Spied on me as I dressed or showered at school (e.g., in a dorm, in a gym, etc.)	6. In a dorm or student housing	6. A dean
7. Flashed or "mooned" me	7. Outside on campus grounds	7. A coach
8. Touched, grabbed, or pinched me in a sexual way	8. In the library	8. A resident advisor/ dorm advisor

(continued)

Table 3.2   (continued)

9. Intentionally brushed up against me in a sexual way	9. In a professor or teaching assistant's office	9. A security guard
10. Asked me to do something sexual in exchange for giving me something (e.g., a better grade, a recommendation, class notes, etc.)	10. In a college office (e.g., administrative office, work study office, etc.)	10. Another school employee
11. Pulled at my clothing in a sexual way	11. In a fraternity or sorority house	11. Someone else
12. Pulled off or down my clothing	12. Someplace else	
13. Blocked my way, cornered me or followed me in a sexual way		
14. Forced me to kiss him/her		
15. Forced me to do something sexual, other than kissing		

Source: Hill and Silva, 2005.

concerning different kinds of sexual harassment, prod for a variety of social-spatial contexts within colleges and universities, and ask respondents for information about the perpetrator (e.g., student, coach, or professor).

From a multiracial feminist perspective, there are several key advantages of this survey instrument relative to those discussed above. First, implicit in the survey design is the assumption that sexual harassment against college students takes forms that are sometimes similar to, but in many cases different from, sexual harassment experienced by other groups. For example, both the Schedule of Sexist Events and the Drawing the Line surveys include questions about sexual comments or jokes, and both include name calling. However, due to the social organization of college campuses (particularly those that are residential), there are opportunities for sexual harassment in this environment that are not present in other contexts. For example, sexual harassment in the workplace does not often involve the perpetrator spying on someone who is dressing or showering. As Martin and Hummer (1989), and DeSantis (2007) describe, fraternity or sorority houses offer highly sexualized, secluded environments in which particular forms of sexual harassment (e.g., a man forcing a woman to kiss him; a man pulling at a woman's clothing in a sexual way) and other forms of violence against women become almost normative. The questions about sexual harassment within the Drawing the Line survey clearly reflect the particularity of sexual harassment within the context of the college environment.

Secondly, because the Drawing the Line survey was designed for students aged 18 to 24, the measures of sexual harassment it includes are especially tailored for that age group. We see forms of sexual harassment included in this survey (such as sexual harassment on the Internet or in text messages) that reflect the lived experiences of contemporary young adults. And because of this, the survey is able to capture the intersection of gender and sexuality with age.

The survey's focus on sexual harassment, as opposed to gender discrimination or sexism, allows one further advantage. Namely, respondents are not asked to attribute their experiences with harassment to one particular social status. As a result, women who perceive their harassment as having been driven by a combination of factors, for example, as "racialized sexual harassment" (Texeira, 2002) or homophobic-sexual harassment, are not forced to choose whether their experiences were driven by one status more than another.

While an excellent tool for understanding college women's experiences with sexual harassment on campus, the Drawing the Line survey is clearly limited in that it is not designed to assess sexual harassment as experienced by women who are not both "college-aged" and currently enrolled in college. While a valuable instrument for assessing sexual harassment in a particular context, and as experienced by a particular group, the very particularity of the survey instrument and the sample to which it was administered makes it difficult to ascertain how sexual harassment within the college environment compares to sexual harassment in other contexts. In addition, although the survey instrument does capture the intersections of gender and sexuality with age, it does not explicitly address potential racial and ethnic differences in women's experiences with sexual harassment.

As a result of both of these factors, the data collected from the Drawing the Line project are limited in their ability to illustrate what sociologist R. W. Connell (1992, p. 736) calls the "relational character of gender"— the ways in which young women's gendered experiences are related to and derive meaning from other groups' gendered experiences. As Baca Zinn et al. (2007, p. 153) explain, "just as masculinity and femininity each depend on the definitions of the other to produce domination, differences *among* women and *among* men are also created in the context of structured relationships." The report *Drawing the Line* highlights the *particularity* of college students' experiences, but, used by itself, is less helpful for understanding the relationships, inequalities, and social processes that help create and maintain these differences.

Taken together, a multiracial feminist framework encourages us to think through how sexism, discrimination, and harassment may be experienced differently for different groups of women. Social statuses other than gender may influence the likelihood that women experience any particular form of sexism and also the particular types of sexism that individual women encounter. Social-spatial context matters, as the likelihood of experiencing particular forms of sexism is contingent on the social-spatial contexts through which women move. Further, the social-spatial contexts in which women reside are themselves related to women's social statuses (including gender but also including age, class, race, and ethnicity). Finally, while sexism does sometimes occur in isolation from other types of discrimination, it also occurs alongside and in combination with other forms of discrimination. In other words, the mistreatment of women is not always motivated solely by gender prejudices but by racial, ethnic, class, and sexuality-based prejudices as well.

As seen above, many measures of sexism that are currently used in social science research are limited in that they provide only a partial picture of women's experiences with sexism, harassment, and discrimination. All measures have limitations, however. And because resources are limited and sexism is both pervasive and dynamic, no one scale can possibly capture women's diverse experiences with sexist events. The partiality is not, in itself, problematic. What is problematic from a multiracial feminist perspective, however, is that within each survey instrument, and across all three instruments, the experiences of some women are systematically centralized, and others are marginalized. The experiences of some women are understood to represent the experiences of, in many cases, *all* women. As philosopher Elizabeth Spelman argued in her book *Inessential Woman*, in focusing on women "as women," "feminist theory has confused the condition of one group of women with the condition of all" (1988, p. 4). A similar phenomenon may be at work in much of the survey research on sexism.

While Klonoff and Landrine are careful to report that some groups of women "experience more frequent gender discrimination within specific domains" than do other groups (1995, p. 467), many researchers who have subsequently used the SSE and other similar scales have glossed over these differences. Simply adding up respondents' total experiences with discrimination, researchers have obscured women's varied experiences with particular types of sexist events (for example, see Ayres, Friedman, & Leaper, 2009; Klonoff, Landrine, & Campbell, 2000; Sabik & Tylka, 2006). What is perhaps even more problematic is that the SSE, originally designed to capture diverse women's experiences, has been most regularly used to assess college women's experiences with sexism (e.g. Ayres, Friedman, & Leaper 2009; Sabik & Tylka 2006; Klonoff, Landrine, & Campbell, 2000). With such limited questions about workplace discrimination, the GSS arguably gives us even less insight into diverse women's experiences!

Speaking of African American women's experiences with racism and sexism, sociologist Patricia Hill Collins (1990/2000, p. 68) writes, "Intersectionality captures the way in which the particular location of black women in dominant American social relations is unique and in some senses unassimilable into the discursive paradigms of gender and race domination." In a similar way, psychologist Roberta L. Nutt (2004) has drawn attention to the ways in which gender-based prejudices and discrimination affect women differently over the life course. As girls and women mature, their bodies increasingly deviate from the infantilized ideal of femininity. As they age, they spend more or less time within particular institutions (schools, workplaces, homes, medical institutions), and their own positions within each of these institutions change (perhaps from student to teacher, from new employee to manager, from daughter to mother/wife/partner/grandparent). What the above review of these measures makes clear is that our measures of sexism, gender discrimination, and sexual harassment have generally centralized gender and marginalized other systems of difference and inequality. The absence of an intersectional framework limits our potential findings, particularly as it applies to marginalized groups—racial and ethnic minorities, sexual minorities, young and older women. Often, our measures work best for groups that are more privileged and, consequently, help to obscure the experiences of those who are already marginalized.

Re-modeling With Multiracial Feminism: Making the Most of General Surveys

In the previous section, I showed how multiracial feminist theorizing provides a framework for critiquing survey questions concerning sexism, gender discrimination, and sexual harassment. This framework is not, however, simply a tool of critique, and the insights of multiracial feminism are not limited to designing better survey questions. Multiracial feminism can also inform the process by which we analyze existing survey data. Specifically, multiracial feminism's focus on difference and intersecting systems of inequality can help survey researchers construct research models that minimize bias and thus better represent the social world. In more political terms, a multiracial feminist approach can help to recognize the experiences of marginalized groups and can challenge the reproduction of inequality in social science research.

In the remainder of this chapter, I demonstrate one approach for bringing a multiracial feminist framework to survey research on sexism and gender discrimination. As a methodological framework, multiracial feminist theory pushes me to pay particular attention to how gender intersects with other social statuses (e.g. age, marital, and family status) and with other systems of inequality. My analyses are designed and carried out with an eye toward difference, while I simultaneously search for shared experiences and commonalities. Three analytic interventions are key: disaggregating data to uncover difference, creating models that reflect diverse experiences, and situating gender inequality within a broader social context.

To demonstrate the importance of a multiracial feminist framework, I analyze data from the 2002 and 2006 General Social Surveys (GSS), a source commonly used in sociological research and social science research more generally. (In Chapter 4, I show how a multiracial feminist approach might inform data more typical of survey research in psychology and, in Chapter 5, data more characteristic of survey research in women's and gender studies.) In 2002 and 2006, the GSS included a special module focusing on the "Quality of Working Life." The survey was administered to 2,765 individuals in 2002 and 4,510 individuals in 2006, and of those, a subsample of respondents were asked a number of specific questions concerning their work life. Some questions concerned job requirements, such as "How many days per month do you work extra hours beyond your usual schedule?" and "When you work extra hours on your main job, is it mandatory (required by your employer)?" Others were more subjective and tapped how individuals feel about their work. For example, respondents were asked, "Please tell me whether you strongly agree, agree, disagree, or strongly disagree with each of these statements. 'I am proud to be working for my employer.'" And, "My main satisfaction in life comes from work." Also included in this module were questions concerning the relationship between work life and family life (e.g., "How often do the demands of your job interfere with your family life?" and "How often do the demands of your family interfere with your work on the job?") and questions concerning discrimination and harassment in the workplace (e.g., "Do you feel in any way discriminated against on your job because of your gender?" and "In the last 12 months, were you sexually harassed by anyone while you were on the job?"). While I believe a multiracial feminist approach could inform an analysis of any of these issues, it is this latter set of questions—those concerning gender discrimination and sexual harassment at work—that I focus on here.

Disaggregating Data to Highlight Difference

Table 3.3 shows the frequency distribution of two variables, "Do you feel in any way discriminated against on your job because of your gender?" and "In the last 12 months, were you sexually harassed by anyone while you were on the job?" as they intersect with respondents' gender. Individuals' responses were coded into four different categories: (1) "yes," indicating that they had experienced discrimination or harassment; (2) "no," indicating that they had not; (3) "don't know," and (4) "no answer." Table 3.3 includes only those respondents who answered "yes" or "no."[v]

Reading across the top row, we can see that when the data from 2002 and 2006 are combined, 46 men surveyed reported that they felt discriminated on the job because of their gender. This represents 2.8% of men who provided answers to the question ($100* 46/1652 = 2.8\%$). As might be expected, significantly more women ($n = 194$) reported that they had experienced gender discrimination on the job. The percentage of women reporting gender-based discrimination is 4 times higher than that of men. Moving across the table, we see that the percentage of women who report having experienced sexual harassment on the job is also higher—more than double—for women than it is for men. The final two columns indicate the percentage of men and women workers who have experienced gender discrimination or sexual harassment while at work.[vi]

In and of themselves, these statistics reveal an important story about gender and work in the contemporary United States. Despite the gains made by feminists in recent decades, despite substantial changes in gender-related attitudes, despite federal legislation prohibiting workplace discrimination on the basis of gender, more than 1 in 10 women workers feels she is experiencing gender discrimination at work. Sadly, in the first

---

[v] When asked about gender discrimination at work, 12 respondents answered "Don't know" (4 men and 8 women), and 30 people provided no answer (17 men and 13 women). When asked about sexual harassment on the job, 11 respondents answered "Don't know" (3 men and 8 women), and 31 people provided no answer (18 men and 13 women).

[vi] Fifty respondents, 10 men and 40 women, indicated that they had experienced both sexual harassment and gender discrimination at work.

Table 3.3   Simple Crosstab for Gender Discrimination in the Workplace by Gender. Combined data from the 2002 and 2006 General Social Surveys (GSS), full-time and part-time workers.

	"Do you feel in any way discriminated against on your job because of your gender?"		"In the last 12 months, were you sexually harassed by anyone while you were on the job?"		"Have you experienced gender discrimination or sexual harassment on the job?"	
	Men	*Women*	*Men*	*Women*	*Men*	*Women*
Yes	46	194	34	98	70	252
	2.78%	11.14%	2.06%	5.63%	4.24%	14.46%
No	1606	1548	1618	1644	1582	1491
	97.22%	88.86%	97.94%	94.37%	95.76%	85.54%
Total	1652	1742	1652	1742	1652	1743
	100%	100%	100%	100%	100%	100%

years of the 21st century nearly 15% of women workers report having experienced either sexual harassment or gender discrimination in their place of employment.[vii]

But how do experiences with workplace sexual harassment and gender discrimination compare for different groups of women? A multiracial feminist approach encourages us to consider how social statuses other than gender shape women's experiences, both within and outside the workplace. Table 3.4 disaggregates the information presented in the previous table, and it examines the frequency with which women in different racial, ethnic, class, and age groups report experiencing gender discrimination or sexual harassment. Reading across the first row, for example, we see that 15.5% of non-Hispanic white women (that is, 193 of 1,245 women who consider themselves to be both white and non-Hispanic) who were working either full- or part-time reported having experienced gender discrimination or sexual harassment at their place of work. This percentage is slightly higher than the percentage of non-Hispanic black or African American women who report having experienced workplace sexism (14.4%) and is nearly

---

[vii] It is worth noting here that these reports of sexism may not reflect the actual level of discrimination and harassment experienced at the workplace. Some respondents may be discriminated against without their realizing it, while others may perceive actions to be discriminatory when in reality they are not.

Table 3.4   Percentage of Women Respondents Who Report Having Experienced Gender Discrimination or Sexual Harassment in the Workplace Recently. Combined data from the 2002 and 2006 General Social Surveys (GSS), full-time and part-time workers.

Racial-Ethnic Group

Non-Hispanic White	Non-Hispanic Black	Hispanic	Non-Hispanic Other	
15.5%	14.3%	8.0%	8.3%	
(193/1245)	(43/300)	(11/138)	(5/60)	

P-Value for Chi-Square: 0.055

Educational Attainment

Less than High School	High School / GED	Junior College	Bachelor's	Graduate Degree
16.4%	12.1%	17.3%	16.4%	18.4%
(20/122)	(110/909)	(33/191)	(57/347)	(32/174)

P-Value for Chi-Square: 0.063

Respondent's Income Quartile (2002)*

Q1 (Less than $15,000 per year)	Q2 ($15,000 to less than $30,000)	Q3 ($30,000 to less than $50,000)	Q4 (More than $50,000)
8.7%	13.6%	22.0%	22.9%
(19/219)	(33/243)	(42/191)	(24/105)

P-Value for Chi-Square: 0.000

Respondent's Income Quartile (2006)*

Q1 (Less than $20,000)	Q2 ($20,000 to less than $40,000)	Q3 ($40,000 to less than $75,000)	Q4 (More than $75,000)
10.8%	12.7%	19.0%	23.3%
(28/260)	(30/237)	(32/168)	(10/43)

P-Value for Chi-Square: 0.027

Respondent's Age group

18–30	31–45	46–60	61+
16.5%	15.9%	13.0%	7.0%
(67/406)	(101/634)	(74/568)	(9/129)

P-Value for Chi-Square: 0.026

Note: General Social Survey (GSS) 2002 and 2006 (Women working part-time or full-time).

*Note: Income quartiles are based on the distribution of men's and women's personal incomes. There are fewer women in the upper quartiles because women's personal incomes tend to be lower than men's.

double the percentage of Hispanic women (8.0%) who report having experienced gender-based discrimination or sexual harassment.[viii]

The differences across personal income and age are particularly significant (as indicated by the p-value of the chi-square test, which is below 0.05). In 2002, 8.7% of full- or part-time working women who earned less than $15,000 reported that they had experienced either gender discrimination or sexual harassment in their workplace. Women who earned more than $15,000 but less than $30,000 were more likely to report having experienced sexism at work: 13.6% reported that they had experienced either gender discrimination or sexual harassment in their workplace. Even higher levels of sexism were reported by women who earned more: 22% of women who earned $30,000 to $50,000 reported experiencing gender discrimination or sexual harassment, and for women who earned above $50,000, the figure rose to 22.9%. This is the same pattern we see in the 2006 data: as women's personal income rises, the rates of reported gender-based discrimination and sexual harassment at work increase. Similar differences are seen in age groupings, only here it is younger women who report higher levels of workplace gender discrimination and sexual harassment. Of women aged 18 to 30, 16.5% report having experienced gender-based discrimination or sexual harassment at work, compared to 13% of women aged 46 to 50.

Taken as a whole, the results from Table 3.4 suggest some notable differences in women's workplace experiences. While some of the differences in this table may result from differences in women's perceptions of discrimination, the results nonetheless underscore potentially important differences: Either women in different class, racial-ethnic, and age groups are *experiencing* different levels of gender-based discrimination and harassment, or *perceptions* of workplace experiences differ for different groups of women. A third possibility is that both perceptions and experiences differ for women in different groups.

Creating Models That Reflect Diverse Experiences

Table 3.5 presents the results from more complex statistical analyses, which again highlight how different social statuses shape women's experiences with workplace sexism. Whereas the analyses presented in

---

[viii] To assess racial and ethnic differences, I used information from two variables in the GSS. The first, "race," asks respondents, "What race do you consider yourself?" the second, "Hispanic," asks respondents, "Are you Spanish, Hispanic, or Latino/a?"

Table 3.4 examined a series of bivariate relationships (e.g., the relationship between income and gender discrimination or the relationship between age and gender discrimination), the analyses in Table 3.5 are multivariate models, where I examine the relationship among multiple variables simultaneously.[ix]

The independent variables (i.e., those thought to predict or influence sexism in the workplace) are listed in the leftmost column of the table. I examine racial and ethnic differences in women's reports of workplace sexism by comparing three groups of women: (1) women who identify as being white and who do not identify as being Hispanic or Latina; (2) women who identify as black or African American and who do not identify as being Hispanic or Latina; and (3) those who identify as either being Hispanic and/or Latina or as something other than African American or black or white. I examine educational differences by comparing five groups: (1) those who have earned less than a high school degree or General Equivalency Diploma (GED), (2) those whose highest degree is a high school diploma or GED, (3) those whose highest degree is from a junior college, (4) those whose highest degree is a bachelor's degree, and (5) those whose highest degree is a graduate degree. Marital and family status is also included in Table 3.3. I compare three groups of women based on their marital status: (1) those who are currently married or widowed, (2) those who are divorced or separated, and (3) those who have never been married. I also include a dichotomous variable for whether the respondent has one or more children: Respondents who have had at least one child are coded 1, and those who have not are coded 0. Respondents' ages are also included and are measured in years.

In addition to the sociodemographic variables listed above, I also include several independent variables that speak to the context in which women are working. At the most general level, I include a dichotomous variable for whether the respondent is currently living (and mostly likely working) in the southern United States (1 = living in the southern United States, 0 = living in another part of the United States). I also include a measure of respondents' personal incomes (an ordinal variable with seven categories, where higher values indicate higher personal income) and a measure of occupational prestige. Occupational prestige scores are meant to measure the status or prestige attached to various occupations. On the GSS measure of occupational prestige, physicians, for example, have the occupational prestige score of 86, social workers have an occupational prestige score of 52, and sales workers in the apparel industry have a relatively low occupational prestige

---

[ix] For an introduction to multivariate regression analyses, see Allison (1999).

score of 30.[x] Finally, I include a dichotomous variable for whether the respondent is working full-time (coded 1) or part-time (coded 0).[xi]

The dependent variable differs for each of the three models. In Model 1, the dependent variable is a dichotomous variable coded 1 if the respondent reported having experienced either gender discrimination or sexual harassment (or both), and it is coded 0 if the respondent reports having experienced neither gender discrimination nor sexual harassment at work. In Model 2, the dependent variable is coded 1 if the respondent reports having experienced gender discrimination, and is coded 0 if the respondent reports no experiences with gender discrimination at work. Similarly, in Model 3 the dependent variable is coded 1 if the respondent reports having experienced sexual harassment at work in the past 12 months and is coded 0 if the respondent reports no experience with workplace sexual harassment in the past year.

The numbers in the body of Table 3.5 are the exponentiated regression coefficients for logistic regression models.[xii] Statistically significant values *above* 1.0 indicate that higher values on the independent variable increase the likelihood of perceiving sexism at work. Statistically significant values *lower* than 1.0 indicate that higher values on the independent variable decrease the likelihood of having perceived sexism at work. I use the conventional notation of asterisks (*, **, or ***) to denote statistically significant coefficients in the table. If coefficients have no asterisks, this indicates that the independent variable is not a good predictor of sexism, after information from the other variables in the model has been taken into consideration.

Looking at Table 3.5, Model 1 shows the regression coefficients for my analysis of the factors that are associated with experiencing either sexual harassment or gender discrimination at work. In combining information concerning women's experiences with both sexual harassment and gender discrimination, my model makes a similar assumption to that made in the Schedule of Sexist Events survey: Namely, sexual harassment and gender discrimination are both sexist events, and the factors associated with one of these experiences are likely associated with experiencing the other.

---

[x] For women who are working full- or part-time, the correlation between income and prestige is 0.421. See the *General Social Survey Codebook*, Appendix F for information on all occupational prestige scores. Available from http://www.norc.org.

[xi] Respondents who are not currently working are excluded from the analysis.

[xii] The logistic regression models here are *multivariate* models, in which all of the independent variables are included in the analysis simultaneously.

Table 3.5   Logistic Regression of Workplace Sexism on Selected Variables. Exponentiated Regression Coefficients, 2002 and 2006 General Social Surveys (GSS), full-time and part-time workers.

	Model 1: Gender Discrimination or Sexual Harassment	Model 2: Gender Discrimination	Model 3: Sexual Harassment
Race (Reference Group Is Non-Hispanic Whites)			
African American / Black (Non-Hispanic)	.826 (0.220)	.950 (0.244)	.704 (0.333)
Hispanic and Other Racial-Ethnic Groups	0.461** (0.291)	.540 (0.322)	0.375* (0.481)
Age (in Years)	0.980** (0.007)	.993 (0.008)	0.955*** (0.012)
Education (Reference Group Is High School Diploma)			
Less Than High School Degree	1.334 (0.332)	.916 (0.422)	2.257 (0.431)
Junior College Degree	1.342 (0.249)	1.214 (0.277)	1.935 (0.363)
Bachelor's Degree	1.231 (0.217)	1.123 (0.242)	1.734 (0.328)
Graduate Degree	1.346 (0.285)	1.145 (0.313)	1.615 (0.463)
Marital Status (Reference Group Is Married or Widowed)			
Divorced or Separated	2.231*** (0.189)	1.978*** (0.208)	2.859*** (0.305)
Never Married	1.894** (0.218)	1.728* (0.246)	2.263** (0.331)
Child(ren)	1.053 (0.199)	1.058 (0.224)	1.035 (0.298)
Working Full-Time	1.574 (0.238)	1.824* (0.284)	.964 (0.331)

(continued)

Table 3.5   (continued)

	Model 1: Gender Discrimination or Sexual Harassment	Model 2: Gender Discrimination	Model 3: Sexual Harassment
Personal Income	1.194** (0.063)	1.2245** (0.070)	1.197 (0.098)
Occupational Prestige	.997 (0.007)	.999 (0.008)	.991 (0.010)
Currently Living in Southern United States	.804 (0.168)	0.676* (0.192)	1.094 (0.248)
Constant	.117 (0.480)	.044 (0.558)	.150 (0.700)
N	1459	1457	1459

Note: Exponentiated coefficients are presented, standard errors in parentheses.
2002 and 2006 General Social Surveys.

In Model 1, the significant factors appear to be race and ethnicity, age, marital status, and personal income. Moving from the top of the table downward, the first coefficient shows that African American women are equally likely to report experiencing sexual harassment or gender discrimination in the workplace, compared to non-Hispanic white women. (Non-Hispanic white women are the reference group, and the coefficient for being African American is not statistically significant, as indicated by the absence of asterisks.) Women who describe themselves as Hispanic or as being part of a different racial-ethnic group, however, are less than half as likely—0.461 times as likely—to report having experienced sexism at work compared to non-Hispanic white women. Controlling for the other variables in the model, age is also very significant—with each additional year of age decreasing the likelihood that women will report experiencing sexism in the workplace. Education appears to be non-significant, but marital status seems to play a big role. Compared to women who are either currently married or widowed (the reference group), women who are currently divorced or separated are more than twice as likely to report having experienced sexism in the workplace. Women who have never been married are also more likely than their married counterparts to experience sexual harassment or gender discrimination: Compared to women who are married or widowed, women who have never married are 89% more likely to report experiencing sexual harassment or gender discrimination in the workplace. Finally, in this model we also see that personal income has a positive and statistically significant impact on perceived experiences of sexual harassment and/or gender discrimination. Controlling for the other variables in the model, women who earn more are more likely to report having experienced sexism in the workplace.

Without a multiracial feminist framework, it would be reasonable to conclude my analysis with Model 1. The results of this analysis do indicate that social statuses other than gender influence the likelihood of experiencing sexism in the workplace. They point, in particular, to the relevance of age, marital status, personal income, and ethnicity for understanding workplace sexism. A multiracial feminist framework, however, takes this analysis several steps further. It suggests, first, that social statuses influence not only the *likelihood* of an individual experiencing sexism but also the *particular kinds* of sexism that an individual may face. Second, it suggests (or "hypothesizes") that women may experience particular kinds of sexism more or less, depending on the social context. And finally, a multiracial feminist framework encourages me to situate workplace sexism in a broader context of intersecting inequalities. It pushes me to explore how sexism occurs alongside, and in combination with, other types of discrimination.

In keeping with this framework, the next two models in Table 3.5 disaggregate workplace sexism. Model 2 focuses on the predictors of gender discrimination in the workplace and Model 3 focuses specifically on women's recent experiences with sexual harassment. When disaggregated in this way, the story becomes more complex, as some of the factors associated with experiencing gender discrimination also are associated with sexual harassment (and vice versa), but some are not. Reading down the column for Model 2, we again see that marital status plays a significant role in women reporting having experienced gender discrimination. Women who appear to be romantically "available" (both those who have never married and those who are divorced or separated) are much more likely—73% and 98% respectively—to report having experienced gender discrimination at work. Controlling for the other variables in the model, women who are working full-time are more likely to report experiencing gender discrimination than are those who are currently working part-time. Women with higher personal incomes are also more likely to report experiencing gender discrimination than are those with lower personal incomes. Finally, living in the South decreases the likelihood that women will report experiencing gender discrimination: Controlling for other variables, women who live in the South are about two thirds as likely (67.6%) to report experiencing gender discrimination, compared to women living in other parts of the United States.

Model 3 tells a different story about sexual harassment in the workplace. While there were no significant differences among racial and ethnic groups uncovered in Model 2, Model 3 suggests strong ethnic differences. While non-Hispanic white and non-Hispanic African American women report similar levels of sexual harassment in the workplace, working women who identify as Hispanic or Latina or as another racial or ethnic group are much less likely (less than half as likely as non-Hispanic whites) to report having experienced sexual harassment in the workplace in the past year.[xiii] A similar story holds true for age: While age was not a statistically significant predictor of gender discrimination in the workplace, age does seem to affect the likelihood that a woman will experience sexual harassment. For each additional year in age, the likelihood that a woman will report experiencing sexual harassment decreases by 5% (100%–95%). Marital status, however, seems to work similarly for gender discrimination and sexual harassment: Compared to women who are married or widowed, women who have never married are more than twice as likely (2.263 times as likely) to report having experienced sexual harassment at work within the past year. Similarly, working women who are divorced or separated are nearly 3 times as likely (2.859 times) to report experiencing sexual harassment at work, controlling for other variables in the model.[xvi] Finally, unlike in the previous model, personal income, full-time participation in the workforce, and living in the southern United States are all statistically *non-significant*, meaning that once the other variables in the model are taken into consideration, these three characteristics do not help in determining which women are likely to report experiences of sexual harassment in the workplace.

Taken together, these analyses convey a complicated story about sexism at work—one that connects women's family lives with their workplace experiences, one that highlights differences across ethnic and age groups but similarities among women despite differences in educational attainment.

[xiii] Welsh, Carr, MacQuarrie, and Huntley (2006) have argued that women of different racial and citizenship statuses define sexual harassment in different ways. Whether the ethnic differences that emerge in Model 3 result from differing experiences or perceptions, the intersectional analysis suggests that these differences shape women's reports of sexual harassment more than women's reports of gender discrimination. See also Essed (2001).

[xiv] Texeria (2002) reports a similar marriage effect when she investigates sexual harassment of African American women in law enforcement. Kohlman's (2006) analysis of the 1994 and 1996 General Social Survey finds that women who are divorced or separated are likely to experience more sexual harassment than do married women but finds no statistically significant difference between women who are married and those who have never married.

Model 2 paints a picture of who is likely to report having experienced gender discrimination at work: women who are working full-time, women who are earning relatively high incomes, and women who are divorced, who are separated, or who have never been married. Who is relatively less likely to report having experienced gender discrimination at work? Women who are working part-time, women with relatively lower incomes, and women who are married. Women currently living in the South are also much less likely to report having experienced gender discrimination, though this may stem from regional differences in gender ideology.

Model 3 presents a different picture—one that focuses on age, in addition to marital status and ethnicity. In brief, young women who are unmarried are more likely to report having experienced sexual harassment compared with those who are older and those who are married or widowed. Women who identify as Hispanic or Latina and those who identify as neither white nor African American are much less likely than non-Hispanic white and non-Hispanic black women to report having experienced sexual harassment in the past year. While higher personal income increases the likelihood of experiencing gender discrimination at work, there is no significant income effect for experiences with sexual harassment.

While one must take care not to read beyond the limits of the data, these findings tell a story of the importance of social statuses other than gender for understanding and documenting sexism in the workplace. It may be that women's coworkers view young and unmarried women as "available" and thus sexually harass, threaten, and otherwise mistreat them. It may be that women with high personal incomes have more opportunities for raises and promotion and thus have more opportunities both to experience and to notice gender discrimination and the persistent "glass ceiling." Conversely, the differences may reflect differences in perceptions of sexism: It may be that unmarried women are more dependent on their careers than are married women; thus, they are less able to minimize mistreatment or harassment in the workplace. In any case, what is clear is that there are some important differences that emerge when women's experiences with sexual harassment are disentangled from their experiences with gender discrimination. Women's social statuses help to determine not only the likelihood that they will encounter sexism in the workforce but also the particular forms of sexism that they encounter.

Situating Gender Within a Broader Social Context

Because sexism occurs alongside and in combination with other systems of inequality, my final analyses in this chapter explore the factors associated with other forms of women's mistreatment at work. And these other forms of mistreatment, though not unique to women, are clearly important to consider when assessing women's experiences at work. While 14.46 % of working women surveyed reported that they had experienced either sexual harassment or gender discrimination at work, 5.4% reported experiencing racial discrimination (among racial- and ethnic-minority women the figure is 12.1%), 8.8% reported experiencing discrimination based on their age, and 11.2% reported experiencing some other type of harassment or threatening behavior in the past 12 months. In total, 27.7% of working women reported experiencing at least one kind of discrimination or harassment at their workplace.

Table 3.6 follows the same format as the previous multivariate models but investigates three different kinds of mistreatment: discrimination based on race or ethnicity, discrimination based on age, and other kinds of threatening or harassing behavior.[xv] As one might expect, Model 1 suggests that racial- and ethnic-minority women are more likely to report having experienced racial or ethnic discrimination than were non-Hispanic white women. African American women were the most likely to report having experienced racial discrimination (nearly 6 times more likely, as compared to non-Hispanic white women) and women who describe themselves as Hispanic or some other racial-ethnic group were more than twice as likely as non-Hispanic white women to report having experienced racial or ethnic discrimination. A very different pattern emerges for age discrimination. Here, younger and older women are more likely than their middle-aged counterparts to report having experienced age discrimination. Controlling for other factors, women aged 18 to 30 were more than 4 times as likely as middle-aged women (aged 31–60) to report having been discriminated against on the basis of age. Older women were also more likely to report age discrimination, as are women who are working full-time (as opposed to part-time), women who are divorced or separated (as opposed to married), and women with advanced educational degrees. For "other kinds" of harassment, the only significant predictor in the model is marital status. Compared to women who are married, women who have never married are 62.9% more likely to report experiencing "other" types of harassment or threatening behavior at work.

[xv] Respondents were asked, "Do you feel in any way discriminated against on your job because of your race or ethnic origin?" Do you feel in any way discriminated against on your job because of your age?" and "In the last 12 months, were you threatened or harassed in any other way by anyone while you were on the job?"

| Table 3.6 | Logistic Regression of Workplace Discrimination and Harassment on Selected Variables. Exponentiated Regression Coefficients, *2002 and 2006 General Social Surveys (GSS)*, full-time and part-time workers. |

	Racial or Ethnic Discrimination	Age Discrimination	Other Kinds of Harassment
Race (Reference Group Is Non-Hispanic Whites)			
African American / Black (Non-Hispanic)	6.919*** (0.295)	.944 (0.283)	.684 (0.259)
Hispanic and Other Racial-Ethnic Groups	2.668* (0.390)	.630 (0.333)	.750 (0.284)
Age (Reference Group Is Aged 31–60)			
Young Women (Aged 18–30)	.943 (0.342)	4.212*** (0.243)	1.157 (0.229)
Older Women (Older Than 60)	1.866 (0.517)	3.604*** (0.351)	.750 (0.392)
Education (Reference Group Is High School Diploma)			
Less Than High School Diploma	.429 (0.630)	1.163 (0.381)	1.015 (0.378)
Junior College Degree	.951 (0.448)	.816 (0.388)	1.264 (0.272)
Bachelor's Degree	.972 (0.381)	1.214 (0.278)	.903 (0.252)
Graduate Degree	1.523 (0.463)	2.183* (0.357)	1.617 (0.297)
Marital Status (Reference Group Is Married or Widowed)			
Divorced or Separated	1.474 (0.308)	2.415*** (0.254)	1.190 (0.213)
Never Married	1.694 (0.344)	1.670 (0.267)	1.629* (0.243)
Child(ren)	1.373 (0.338)	.831 (0.244)	1.395 (0.230)

(Continued)

Table 3.6   (continued)

	Racial or Ethnic Discrimination	Age Discrimination	Other Kinds of Harassment
Working Full-time	1.841	2.026*	1.157
	(0.420)	(0.289)	(0.238)
Personal Income	1.179	.945	1.096
	(0.109)	(0.086)	(0.071)
Occupational Prestige	.983	.993	1.001
	(0.011)	(0.009)	(0.008)
Currently Living in Southern United States	1.138	.672	.931
	(0.264)	(0.217)	(0.183)
Constant	.012	.040	.057
	(0.701)	(0.510)	(0.446)
Number of Respondents in Each Model	1,458	1,458	1,459

Note: Exponentiated coefficients are presented, standard errors in parentheses. 2002 and 2006 General Social Surveys. Working women only.

Conclusion

Taken as a whole, the analyses presented in this chapter help illustrate the importance of a multiracial feminist or intersectional approach to understanding and analyzing sexism. Drawing from multiracial feminist theorizing, I argued at the beginning of this chapter that multiracial feminism offered important and underused insights for survey research on sexism. In particular, I suggested that social statuses other than gender influence the likelihood that women experience sexism, as well as the particular kind of sexism that women experience. In addition, I argued that women's experiences with sexism are shaped by the social-spatial contexts in which women reside and that it was important to consider sexism as occurring alongside and in combination with other forms of discrimination.

The above analyses lend support to each of these claims and, in so doing, reveal the potential limitations of survey research that ignore issues of intersectionality. A multiracial feminist approach highlights the benefits of disaggregating index variables—analyzing the predictors of particular forms of sexism rather than analyzing the predictors of sexism in general—because the predictors of particular forms of sexism themselves may vary. A multiracial feminist approach also highlights the importance of examining sexism within diverse social-spatial contexts, as well as in the broader context of intersecting systems of inequality.

Comparing Table 3.6 with those presented earlier, we can see some interesting similarities and differences. That the significant predictors of particular forms of mistreatment vary shows that some groups perceive more experiences with particular forms of discrimination and harassment than others. That there are some consistencies across tables in the predictors of mistreatment suggests the possibility of intersecting forms of discrimination. Young women (aged 18–30), for example, are the most likely age group to report age discrimination. Younger women are most likely to report sexual harassment, and sexual harassment is also tied to marital status. Those studies that have included sexual harassment as one of many indicators of sexism, risk obscuring the ways in which age and marital status shape women's experiences. Without systematic attention to the diversity of women's experiences and the social statuses that shape these experiences, our analyses risk making claims about "gender discrimination" or "women" that reflect only *some* women's experiences. As Elizabeth Spelman (1988, p. 159) writes of feminist theory,

> [t]hose who produce the "story of woman" want to make sure they appear in it. The best way to ensure that is to be the storyteller and hence to be in a position to decide which of all the many facts about women's lives ought to go into the story, which ought to be left out. Essentialism works well in behalf of these aims, aims that subvert the very process by which women might come to see where and how they wish to make common cause. For essentialism invites me to take what I understand to be true of me "as a woman" for some golden nugget of womanness all women have as women; and it makes the participation of other women inessential to the production of the story. How lovely: the many turn out to be one, and the one that they are is me.

From a multiracial feminist perspective, the participation of diverse women and men is essential to the production of the story. Diversity of experiences and perspectives should be evident in the theories that inform our research, in our statistical analyses, and also in our interpretations of our results. Because these experiences and perspectives are found outside traditional social science canons, incorporating a multiracial feminist perspective will require an interdisciplinary approach. As we will see in the next two chapters, an interdisciplinary multiracial feminist approach is important not only for understanding and analyzing sexism but also for understanding and analyzing racism and feminism.

4

Further Re-modeling With Multiracial Feminism

Highlighting Interactive Effects of Race, Ethnicity, Age, and Gender

> "Note that not only Black women but also Black men are confronted with racism structured by racist constructions of gender roles, notable examples being the absent father stereotype or the myth of the Black rapist" (Duster, 1970, and Hernton, 1965, qtd. in Essed).
>
> ~Philomena Essed 1991, p. 31

Introduction

In the previous chapter I argued that multiracial feminism offers a fruitful yet underused theoretical perspective from which to analyze sexism and gender discrimination. While previous research on sexism has yielded valuable information, I suggested that, by focusing primarily on *gender*, scholars had obscured how other social statuses—such as age, race, ethnicity, and class—interacted with gender to shape women's experiences. Using data from the General Social Survey (GSS), I showed how even with minimal measures of sexism, a multiracial feminist approach could highlight important commonalities and differences among women. In this chapter, I hope to show how a multiracial feminist approach can similarly inform survey research on racial discrimination. Just as survey research on sexism and gender discrimination has focused primarily on one dimension of inequality (gender), so too has research on racial discrimination (race). While attention to race is clearly important for analyzing racial discrimination, a multiracial feminist perspective highlights how racial inequalities work with and through other systems of inequality to shape the experiences of all individuals. While not discounting the importance of previous work, I hope to bring attention to the potential contributions of an interdisciplinary multiracial feminist or "intersectional" approach for this area of research.

Building on the insights presented in the previous two chapters, this chapter focuses on issues of measurement bias and universalizing models in survey research on racial discrimination. Whereas the previous chapter analyzed data from a general social survey to highlight experiences of discrimination, this chapter draws on data from a more particular survey: the 2001 to 2003 National Survey of American Life (NSAL): Coping With Stress in the 21st Century. While the General Social Survey is designed to understand a range of social issues, the NSAL is designed specifically to "gather data about the physical, emotional, mental, structural, and economic conditions of black Americans" (http://www.rcgd.isr.umich.edu/prba/nsal). In addition, where as the previous chapter developed an intersectional approach to analyzing the *predictors* of workplace sexism and discrimination more generally this chapter demonstrates how an intersectional approach can illuminate some of the *consequences* of discrimination. Like research on feminism and sexism, survey research on racial and ethnic discrimination can be classified into three broad groups: studies that analyze data from large general social surveys, studies that use data from surveys that are more focused yet still include large samples, and studies that use smaller surveys designed to understand a particular phenomenon in a particular context. In this chapter, I demonstrate how a multiracial feminist approach can inform survey research that falls within the second category: the NSAL is focused rather than general, yet it includes a large and diverse sample of respondents.

Situating Racial Discrimination Within a Multiracial Feminist Framework

As discussed in the previous chapter, one of the central claims of multiracial feminist theory is that all individuals occupy multiple social statuses: a racial and ethnic status, a gender status, class and age statuses, as well as others. Multiracial feminist theories emphasize how the interplay of these social statuses affects the lives of all individuals, even when individuals are themselves not cognizant of these intersecting statuses. And just as multiracial feminist theories of simultaneity offer important and underused insights into sexism and gender, these same theories shed light on the complexity of racial and ethnic discrimination.

In our work on gendered racial discrimination, Mosi Ifatunji and I suggested that multiracial feminist theorizing offers a useful perspective from which to understand race and racism as they intersect with other systems of inequality (Harnois & Ifatunji, 2011). One important insight, as Essed highlights in the quotation opening this chapter, concerns the particular forms of prejudice and discrimination that racial minorities encounter. Both black women and black men must contend with a number of racial stereotypes, but many of these racial stereotypes are also deeply gendered. And, in addition to being gendered, racial stereotypes often draw on age-specific, class-based, and sexualized prejudices. The stereotype of the "welfare queen," for example, is not only a racial stereotype but also one based on class (lower class), gender (women), and sexuality (hypersexual). The same holds true for the contemporary stereotype of the criminal, or "thug"—typically portrayed as black, lower class, male, hypersexual, and often young (see Hill Collins, 2004; hooks, 2004; Kelley, 1995).[i] While some racial and ethnic stereotypes might be applied equally to men and women, multiracial feminist theories underscore the importance of considering how some racial and ethnic stereotypes are structured by multiple intersecting hierarchies. As with "sexist events," multiracial feminist theories challenge us to broaden our notions of *racial stereotypes* and *racial discrimination* to include those that reflect intersecting systems of inequality. A multiracial feminist approach to survey research on racial discrimination requires researchers to address the possibility of gendered, classed, age-specific, and sexualized racial stereotypes and discriminatory practices in our analyses.

---

[i] While Hill Collins's work is qualitative and largely theoretical, a number of recent empirical studies have documented the pervasiveness of gendered-racial stereotypes. Timberlake and Estes (2007), for example, investigated whether Black women and Black men were stereotyped in different ways and found that in many cases racial stereotypes were related to gender. Analyzing survey data from the 1992–1994 Multi-City Study of Urban Inequality, they found that "whites rated black men significantly lower than black women on the criminality stereotype." Black women, in contrast, were more likely to be stereotyped as less self-sufficient (i.e., more dependent on social welfare) than were black men (2007, p. 417). In another recent study Shih (2002) explored the racial and ethnic stereotypes held by employers and found that their stereotypes were similarly gendered: Black women were often stereotyped as "single mothers or as 'matriarchs,'" and black men were stereotyped as being more hostile and angry (2002, p. 111).

A second insight from multiracial feminism concerns the importance of considering multiple reference groups when understanding and operationalizing racial discrimination. Forty years ago, Francis Beale wrote of the "double jeopardy" that black women faced in a society marked by both racism and sexism (Beale, 1970). More recently, multiracial feminist scholars have expanded this notion, writing of *multiple jeopardies* (King, 1988)—a concept meant to highlight intersecting and multiplicative systems of inequality. King (1988, pp. 47–48) explains the importance of this theoretical shift by considering the sexual exploitation of black women during slavery:

> While black women workers suffered the same demanding physical labor and brutal punishments as black men, as females, we were also subject to forms of subjugation only applicable to women. Angela Davis, in *Women, Race and Class*, notes, "If the most violent punishments of men consisted in floggings and mutilations, women were flogged and mutilated, as well as raped." At the same time, our reproductive and child-rearing activities served to enhance the quantity and quality of the "capital" of a slave economy. Our institutionalized exploitation as the concubines, mistresses, and sexual slaves of white males distinguished our experience from that of white females' sexual oppression because it could only have existed in relation to racist and classist forms of domination.
>
> *The importance of any one factor in explaining black women's circumstances thus varies depending on the particular aspect of our lives under consideration and the reference groups to whom we are compared.* [Italics added for emphasis]

In this passage, King demonstrates the importance of using multiple reference groups to understand the historical oppression of black women. A single-oppression framework that focuses on racial inequality highlights some important aspects of racism: economic exploitation, extreme violence and physical abuse, and dehumanization. But an intersectional analysis incorporates some additional dimensions: the sexual abuse of black women under slavery and, more generally, the systematic denial of the protections and privileges associated with femininity to racial-ethnic minority women (see also Essed, 1991; Thornton Dill, 1988). King shows us that understanding the subjugation of women slaves requires considering how race, gender, and sexuality intersect to shape the conditions of their lives.

Studies of racism or sexism that seek to understand black women's experiences by looking through the lens of racism *or* sexism can yield valuable insights. But such a framework at best captures only one partial dimension of black women's experiences. A multiracial feminist approach, in contrast, encourages us to examine the multiplicative effects of race and gender in the lives of racial minority women, and doing so requires comparing black women's experiences with (at least) two reference groups: whites in general and white women in particular.

In addition to emphasizing intersecting social statuses and multiple axes of inequality, multiracial feminist theories highlight the importance of considering the social-spatial contexts in which individuals experience racial discrimination. Just as we saw with gender discrimination, racial discrimination can take different forms in different social-spatial contexts (Feagin, 1991; Feagin & Eckberg, 1980; Roscigno, 2007). And social-spatial contexts are themselves often organized by the intersecting hierarchies of gender, race, class, and sexuality. By drawing attention to individual-level statuses and social-spatial contexts, multiracial feminist theories highlight the importance of considering macrolevel and microlevel intersections and the relationship between the two. For it to be consistent with multiracial feminist theory, survey research on racial discrimination must address these intersections in both survey measures as well as statistical models.

While there are no doubt other ways in which multiracial feminism can inform survey research, the final theme I consider here concerns how individuals respond to, and are affected by, particular forms of discrimination. Multiracial feminist theories emphasize that people in different social locations often respond to events in different ways. As Paula Moya explains, "as long as our world is hierarchically organized along enduring relations of domination, people occupying different social locations will tend to experience the world in systematically different ways; . . . not everyone who has the same kind of experience will react in the same way or come to the same conclusions about that experience" (2001, p. 472). If it is to be compatible with multiracial feminism, social science research (both quantitative and qualitative) requires us to address this possibility explicitly in our analyses. For as I hope to show in this chapter, if this possibility is not addressed explicitly, then our models may obscure the very relationships we seek to clarify in our research.

Re-modeling With Multiracial Feminism: Making the Most of Multiple Measures

In our previous work, Ifatunji and I analyzed the most commonly used measures of racial discrimination in the social sciences and found that few explicitly took gender differences into account.[ii] While some measures of racial discrimination did allude to gendered racial stereotypes, most did not. Those that did typically mentioned gendered-racial stereotypes that applied to *men*. For example, the Index of Race-Related Stress

---

[ii] See Harnois and Ifatunji (2011); for a recent exception, see Thomas, Witherspoon and Speight (2008).

(IRRS) includes 46 items that tap respondents' experience with racial discrimination, but of these, only four suggest gender differences.[1] Each of the four imply racial discrimination targeted at black men rather than black women: "You have heard reports of white people/non-blacks who have committed crimes, and in an effort to cover up their deeds falsely reported that a black man was responsible for the crime"; "You have heard it suggested that black men have an uncontrollable desire to possess a white women"; "You have observed that White kids who commit violent crimes are portrayed as 'boys being boys,' while black kids who commit similar crimes are wild animals"; and "You notice that the media plays up those stories that cast blacks in negative ways (child abusers, rapists, muggers, etc., [or as savages] Wild Man of 96th Street, Wolf pack, etc.), usually accompanied by a large picture of a black person looking angry or disturbed." In emphasizing men's experiences with discrimination, the IRRS contributes to what psychologists Purdie-Vaughns and Eibach (2008) refer to as "intersectional invisibility"—the general failure to fully recognize people with multiple marginal identities (e.g., black women) as "members of their constituent groups."

In addition to relying on gendered *measures* of racial discrimination, the vast majority of survey research on racial discrimination uses *models* of racial discrimination that prevent potential gender difference from emerging. For example, Sellers, Caldwell, and Schmeelk-Cone (2003) investigate how racial discrimination, perceived stress, and racial identity influence and affect psychological well-being among young African American adults, but they incorporate no analysis of how racial discrimination or its relationship to psychological well-being might be shaped by gender. In their interviews, they ask respondents about 20 kinds of discriminatory acts, but they refrain from including any analysis of gender difference; nor do they include gender as a control variable in their analysis. Their model reveals an important relationship between discrimination, identity, and well-being, but it says very little about how these relationships may (or may not) be shaped by gender.

Several recent studies of racial discrimination (e.g., Broman, Mavaddat, & Hsu, 2000; Forman, Williams, & Jackson, 1997; Sellers & Shelton, 2003) have included gender as one of several control variables, but this approach too has important limitations. When gender is included as a simple dichotomous variable within the context of a multivariate regression analysis, it allows the researcher to determine whether men and women tend to differ on the dependent variable, once information from other variables is taken into consideration. This approach to modeling, however, limits the potential for understanding the indirect effects of gender—the ways in which gender may mediate the relationships between the dependent variable and other independent variables in the model.

---

[1] See Utsey and Ponterotto (1996).

In this chapter, I seek to build on previous statistical studies of racial and ethnic discrimination by bringing a multiracial feminist perspective to this research. Such a perspective, I argue, is an important tool for critiquing existing research and an equally important tool for designing research that is sensitive to difference and inequality. As in the previous chapter, I use multiracial feminist theory as a methodological framework and explore the implications of this framework for understanding racial and ethnic discrimination. As a methodological framework, multiracial feminist theory pushes me to pay particular attention to how race and ethnicity intersect with other social statuses (e.g., gender, age, marital and family status) and with other systems of inequality. My analyses are designed and carried out with an eye toward difference, while I simultaneously search for shared experiences and commonalities.

My data come from the 2001 to 2003 National Survey of American Life: Coping With Stress in the 21st Century (NSAL). The NSAL conducted face-to-face interviews with African American, Afro-Caribbean, Hispanic, and non-Hispanic white respondents who were 18 years of age or older living in "urban and rural centers of the country where significant numbers of black Americans reside" (http://www.rcgd.isr.umich.edu/prba/nsal). Because the survey is designed to gather data about the experiences of black Americans, it includes a large number of questions that assess discrimination and mistreatment. The questions it includes are very specific and deliberately tap a wide range of experiences—especially when compared to those included in the GSS.

The analyses I present here focus on two types of discrimination. The first, *major-life* discrimination, includes experiences of mistreatment that, when experienced even once, may negatively impact one's well-being and ability to succeed in life. In the NSAL, major-life discrimination is assessed with nine event-specific questions, including, "For unfair reasons, have you ever not been hired for a job?"; "Have you ever been unfairly denied a promotion?"; "At any time in your life, have you ever been unfairly fired?"; "Have you ever been unfairly prevented from moving into a neighborhood because the landlord or a realtor refused to sell or rent you a house or apartment?"; "Have you ever moved into a neighborhood where neighbors made life difficult for you or your family?"; "Have you ever been unfairly discouraged by a teacher or advisor from continuing your education?"; "Have you ever been unfairly stopped, searched, questioned, physically threatened or abused by the police?"; "Have you been unfairly denied a bank loan?"; and "Have you ever received service from someone such as a plumber or car mechanic that was worse than what other people get?" After each of these questions, respondents were asked to identify the perceived cause of this mistreatment (for example, their race, gender, ancestry).

The second type of discrimination that I investigate is *everyday* discrimination. In contrast to major-life discrimination, everyday discrimination encompasses the mistreatment that individuals face in day-to-day life. It is assessed with 10 questions: "In your day-to-day life, how often have any of the following things happened to you? . . . you are treated with less courtesy than other people?"; "you are treated with less respect than other people?"; "you receive poor service compared with other people at restaurants or stores?"; "people act as if they think you are not smart?"; "people act as if they are afraid of you?"; "people act as if they think you are dishonest?"; "people act as if they're better than you are?"; "you are called names or insulted?"; "you are threatened or harassed?"; and "you are followed around in stores?" Items that tap everyday discrimination were recoded into six categories, where 1 represents not having experienced a particular type of discrimination and 6 indicates having experienced this mistreatment "almost every day." My analysis of everyday discrimination differs from my analysis of major-life discrimination in that it includes information concerning the frequency of mistreatment. It is simultaneously limited, however, by the lack of information concerning the perceived cause of the respondent's mistreatment.

Disaggregating Data to Highlight Difference

Figure 4.1 shows the percentage of respondents who report having ever experienced particular forms of major-life discrimination. Included in these percentages are respondents who attribute the cause of this mistreatment to a variety of individual characteristics, including race, ethnicity, gender, age, height or weight, or sexual orientation (among others). For example, 24% of African Americans sampled report having been unfairly stopped, searched, questioned, physically threatened, or abused by the police.

The next figure disaggregates the information presented in Figure 4.1, focusing on the role of gender in major-life discrimination. As in the previous table, the percentages presented in Figure 4.2 represent those respondents who attribute the cause of their mistreatment to a number of characteristics, including, but not limited to, race and ethnicity. Within each graph, the bars on the left correspond to men's experiences with discrimination, and the bars on the right focus on women. When comparing perceptions of discrimination in this way, one thing stands out immediately: Men tend to report more experiences with discrimination than do women. This is true if we compare gender differences within racial-ethnic groups, as shown below, and when the data are aggregated across racial and ethnic groups. For example, 24% of African American respondents reported mistreatment

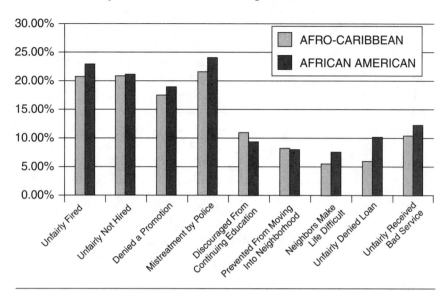

Figure 4.1 Percent of Afro-Caribbean and African Americans Who Perceive Major-Life Discrimination.

Note: From *National Survey of American Life (NSAL), 2001–2003*.

by the police (Figure 4.1), but Figure 4.2 shows that this experience—or at the very least *perceptions* of this experience—are deeply gendered. Forty five Percentage of African American men report mistreatment by the police, compared to 12.6% of African American women. A similar, though not as drastic, pattern occurs with most of the other variables. Men of each racial-ethnic group are more likely to report negative experiences at work: having been not offered a job, unfairly fired, or denied a promotion. Within this broad trend, one major exception stands out: For those instances of major-life discrimination involving housing and education, the percentages of women and men reporting mistreatment is quite similar.

Comparing the information presented in Figures 4.1 and 4.2 highlights the limitations of presenting aggregated data for men and women. Because women's and men's reported experiences with discrimination are so disparate, the aggregated information obscures *both men's and women's* experiences. But a multiracial feminist approach pushes us to consider how *multiple* intersecting statuses shape individuals' experiences—not just race, ethnicity, and gender. The next table presents similar information but this time is further disaggregated by age in addition to race, ethnicity, and gender. Unlike in the previous figures, Table 4.3 is limited to experiences with perceived *racial and ethnic* discrimination. In the NSAL, respondents were asked a follow-up question for each type of major-life discrimination: "What

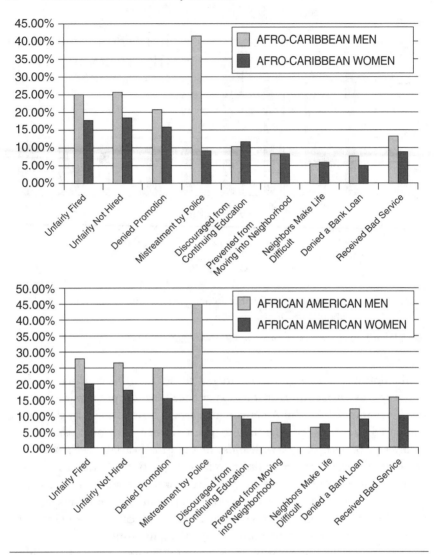

Figure 4.2   Major-Life Discrimination by Ethnicity and Gender.

Note: From *National Survey of American Life (NSAL), 2001–2003.*

do you think was the main reason for this experience?" If respondents attributed their mistreatment to their "skin color," race, ancestry, or origins, they were coded 1 for having experienced major-life racial-ethnic discrimination. Respondents were coded 0 if they (1) reported not having experienced a particular type of mistreatment, (2) attributed this mistreatment to something else (e.g., their gender, age, weight, medical condition, sexual orientation, income), or (3) were unsure of the cause of their mistreatment.

When perceptions of major-life racial and ethnic discrimination are analyzed in this way, a number of interesting things stand out. First, we can see that, within each racial, ethnic, and gender category, there are noticeable differences with respect to age. For example, young men— particularly those between the ages of 18 and 30—are much more likely than their older counterparts to report having been mistreated by the police. The opposite pattern occurs for mistreatment within work-related settings: Older men are more likely to report having been denied a promotion or not having been hired for reasons related to race or ethnicity. Still a third pattern occurs when we analyze women's experiences. While for men, the age trend within each cluster of bars tends to move either upward or downward with age, we see a different trend with respect to age differences among African American and Afro-Caribbean women. When we look at the clusters of three bars for women, we see that the middle bar—that representing women who are aged 31 to 60 tends to be higher than that for either younger or older women. For example, roughly 10% of African American women aged 31 to 60 report experiencing racial-ethnic discrimination in hiring, while less than 8% of women aged 18 to 30 and roughly 4% of African American aged 61 and older report this experience. In other words, the relationship between age group and racial-ethnic discrimination appears to be mediated by gender.

In addition to revealing the intersection of age with gender, the above graphs suggest that contextual differences might be gendered as well. In Figure 4.2, we saw that gender differences in reports of discrimination were greater in some domains (e.g., work–life) than in others (e.g., community life and education). Figure 4.3 complicates the idea of gendered contexts even further. Among men—both African American and Afro-Caribbean—experiences with racial- and ethnic-discrimination vary widely based on social-spatial contexts. In their work lives and in their encounters with the police, men report high levels of racial-ethnic discrimination, and while they also report experiences with discrimination in their community lives, their reports of racial-ethnic discrimination in this context are significantly smaller. (Compare, for example, the left half of the graph for Afro-Caribbean men with the right half.). Women's reports of discrimination also depend on the social-spatial context, but the differences are not as extreme. (For example, compare the left half of the graph for Afro-Caribbean women with the right half.) While it still appears that men report more experiences with major-life racial and ethnic discrimination than do women (note that the Y-axis is scaled differently in each of the graphs), gender and age clearly play important—and complex—roles in shaping individuals' experiences with racial and ethnic discrimination.

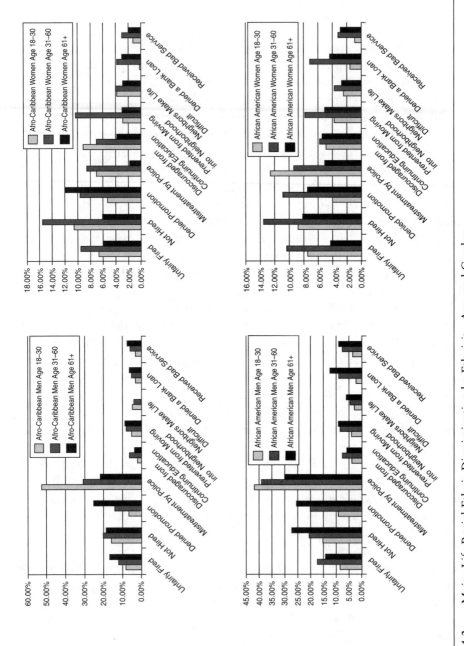

Figure 4.3 Major-Life Racial-Ethnic Discrimination by Ethnicity, Age, and Gender.
Note: From *National Survey of American Life (NSAL), 2001–2003*.

Creating Multiplex Models via Split Samples

The next part of my analysis investigates the relationship between discrimination and individual well-being. The existing literature on the consequences of interpersonal discrimination is vast and spans a number of academic disciplines, including sociology, psychology, racial and ethnic studies, and public health. And while survey-based studies of racial-ethnic discrimination almost always include some discussion of gender, few have systematically addressed the ways in which individuals' *experiences* with racial-ethnic discrimination and their *responses* to particular forms of discrimination may be linked to gender, age, and class. As mentioned above, multiracial feminist theories suggest that racial minority men and women often face different kinds of discrimination and experience this mistreatment in different social-spatial contexts. In addition, a multiracial feminist perspective highlights how individuals' responses to discrimination may depend in part on their location within the intersecting hierarchies of gender, class, sexuality, and age. I argued above that survey research has typically relied on generic measures of racial discrimination that ultimately obfuscate the differences in men's and women's experiences. So too has survey research generally relied on statistical *models* that assume that racial discrimination affects women and men in exactly the same way.[iii]

To illustrate this idea further, I use data from the 2001–2003 National Survey of American Life to assess how perceived discrimination affects individuals' self-satisfaction. My analysis is limited to respondents who describe themselves as being either Afro-Caribbean or African American. Self-satisfaction is measured with a four-category, ordinal-level variable, where higher values indicate greater *dissatisfaction*. Respondents were asked whether they strongly agreed, somewhat agreed, somewhat disagreed, or strongly disagreed with the following statement, "I am satisfied with myself." The majority of respondents, both men and women, responded that they "strongly agreed" with this statement, and roughly a quarter of respondents indicated that they only "somewhat agreed."

I begin by investigating the relationship between instances of major-life racial discrimination and overall self-satisfaction. In the next set of analyses, I explore the impact of "everyday" discrimination on self-satisfaction. In both analyses, I use ordinal logistic regression models, because the dependent variable (self-satisfaction) has four ordered categories. The independent variables

---

[iii] For exception, see Kessler, Mickelson, and Williams (1999), who use interaction terms to capture some aspects of gendered racism, and Caldwell, Guthrie, and Jackson (2006), who run separate regression models to capture some aspects of intersectionality.

in the models include ethnic group (Afro-Caribbean vs. African American), educational attainment, age group, household income, marital status, and gender. In addition, because respondents' racial attitudes might affect individuals' perceptions of discrimination, as well as their self-satisfaction, I control for this characteristic using the question, How true is it that blacks are hardworking? I begin with nine separate models, where each model includes all of the aforementioned control variables as well as one variable indicating whether the respondent has experienced a particular form of racial discrimination.

For example, Model 1 includes all of the control variables, as well as an independent variable assessing whether the respondent perceives having been unfairly fired due to her or his race, ethnicity, or ancestry. The asterisks indicate statistical significance or level of confidence in the coefficient. For example, the 1.297** indicates that when other variables in the model are held constant, individuals who perceive themselves as having been unfairly fired due to their race or ethnicity are more likely to be highly dissatisfied compared to those who have not experienced this type of discrimination. Reading down "Total Sample" Column, we can see that in seven of the nine models, instances of racial discrimination are significantly associated with respondents' self-satisfaction. In all of the models, the effects of discrimination are in the same direction. The exponentiated regression coefficients, or odds ratios, with values greater than 1.0 suggest that perceptions of having experienced major-life discrimination increase the likelihood of higher levels of self-dissatisfaction. Interestingly, in all but one model, Model 4, the effects of the respondents' gender are non-significant (results not shown). Modeling racial discrimination and self-satisfaction in this way, the results suggest that racial discrimination has strong effects on individuals' self-satisfaction, but gender plays a much more limited role.

A more interesting and complicated story emerges when the modeling strategy is revised with an intersectional approach. As previously mentioned, a multiracial feminist perspective suggests that gender influences not only what forms of discrimination an individual encounters but also how individuals respond to this mistreatment. In other words, gender may mediate the relationship between particular forms of racial-ethnic discrimination and self-satisfaction. There are several different approaches to statistical modeling with an intersectional approach. One approach is to conduct separate regression analyses for different groups, in this case for men and women. Modeling racial discrimination in this way allows me to investigate how the correlates of self-satisfaction (including racial discrimination) may affect men's and women's self-satisfaction in different ways. Compared with Models 1 through 10, this approach makes fewer assumptions about the similarities between men and women and thus is more consistent with a multiracial feminist approach.

The right half of Table 4.1 shows the results of my ordinal logistic regression models, this time using a split sample. Whereas the previous approach included gender as a dichotomous independent variable, in this second approach I conduct separate regression analyses for men and women. Because there is no gender variation within each subsample, gender is no longer included as an independent variable. However, by comparing the coefficients and significance of the independent variables for men and women, we can gain a more nuanced understanding of how gender may shape the relationship between discrimination and self-satisfaction.[iv]

The results from the split-sample regressions suggest many similarities in men's and women's experiences of racial-ethnic discrimination and self-satisfaction. The statistically significant odds ratios with values greater than 1.0 indicate that individuals—both men and women—who perceive themselves as having been unfairly fired because of their race or ethnicity are more likely to be highly dissatisfied, controlling for other factors, compared with those who have not had this experience. So too are individuals who report having been not hired, prevented from moving into a neighborhood, or mistreated by the police (again because of their racial or ethnic status). Despite these similarities, the split-sample regression models suggest that racial-ethnic discrimination may impact men's and women's self-satisfaction differently. Though African American and Afro-Caribbean men are more likely to report having been denied a promotion because of their race or ethnicity than are African American and Afro-Caribbean women (Figure 4.2), perceptions of racial discrimination in promotion are not significantly linked to men's self-satisfaction, once other factors are controlled for. Comparing both the size of the coefficient and the statistical significance of this variable for men and women suggests that women's experiences with racial and ethnic discrimination in promotion may be more closely linked to women's self-satisfaction than with men's. The same holds true for discrimination in educational contexts. Women who perceive themselves as having been discouraged from continuing their education, again, because of their racial-ethnic status, are more likely to report higher levels of dissatisfaction than women who have not experienced this. This relationship is not statistically significant among men once other variables are taken into consideration. On the other hand, men who perceive that they have received

---

[iv] Splitting the sample by gender and running separate regression models is one basic way to allow gender differences to emerge. An important limitation to this approach, however, is that the resulting models do not allow us to assess whether differences across models are statistically significant. For this reason, many researchers employ interaction terms within the same model, an approach described further on in this chapter.

Table 4.1   Does Racial-Ethnic Discrimination Significantly Affect Individuals' Self-Satisfaction? Exponentiated Coefficients from Ordinal Logistic Regression Models, 2001–2003 *National Survey of American Life (NSAL)*.

	Total Sample	Split Sample	
		Men	Women
	(Models 1–9)	(Models 10–18)	(Models 19–27)
1. Unfairly Fired	1.297**	1.336*	1.265*
2. Unfairly Not Hired	1.385***	1.573***	1.228+
3. Unfairly Denied Promotion	1.280**	1.210	1.326*
4. Mistreatment by Police	1.537***	1.598***	1.495**
5. Discouraged From Education	1.358*	1.196	1.449*
6. Prevented From Moving Into Neighborhood	1.539***	1.465*	1.564**
7. Neighbors Make Life Difficult	1.265	1.327	1.207
8. Denied a Bank Loan	1.069	1.018	1.089
9. Received Bad Service	1.416*	1.592*	1.184

Note: Control variables include gender (only in models 1–9), ethnic group, generation, household income, educational attainment, racial attitudes, and marital status.

Number of cases for men in each model ranges from 1,059 to 1,099. Number of cases for women ranges from 1,720 to 1,780.

* significant at 5%; ** significant at 1%; *** significant at 0.1%, with a two-tailed test.

+ Indicates significance only with a one-tailed, directional test (p < 0.05).

bad service due to their race or ethnicity are more likely to report greater dissatisfaction than those men who have not had this experience. This relationship is not statistically significant, however, among women once other variables are taken into consideration.

This is not to say women suffer from discrimination within educational contexts and men do not or that men suffer from discrimination in the service sector but that women do not. These regressions are looking at only one aspect of individual well-being, and discrimination in both contexts certainly has negative effects for both men and women. What these split-sample regression models do suggest, however, is that some forms of major-life racial-ethnic discrimination may have a greater impact on women's self-satisfaction and other forms may have a larger impact on men's. Still other forms appear to affect men's and women's self-satisfaction in similar ways. While men are much more likely to experience mistreatment by the police, as we saw in Figures 4.2 and 4.3, the regression analyses here suggest that, for both men and women, mistreatment by the police has lasting effects on self-satisfaction.

Creating Multiplex Models via Interaction Terms

As mentioned in the previous chapter, a multiracial feminist approach encourages us to examine the broader context of inequality in which discriminatory acts are experienced. It encourages researchers to view racial discrimination as occurring alongside and in combination with other forms of discrimination and harassment. In the next section of my analysis, I show how gender can mediate the relationship between *general* discrimination (i.e., discrimination on the basis of race, ethnicity, gender sexual orientation, age, or a number of other factors) and self-satisfaction. Again, I use data from the National Survey of American Life, but in this portion of the analysis I examine everyday as opposed to major-life discrimination. Everyday discrimination includes discriminatory actions that one is likely to face in day-to-day interactions with other people—including teachers, colleagues, friends, and strangers. While even one instance of major-life discrimination can derail a person's opportunities for success, the consequences of one instance of everyday discrimination tend to be less severe. However, because instances of everyday discrimination can and do happen with greater frequency, the cumulative impact of this mistreatment can be just as damaging, if not more so.

Table 4.2 presents the mean values for men's and women's perceptions of everyday discrimination. The variable, with values ranging from 1 to 6, measures the frequency with which respondents perceive instances of everyday discrimination based on race, gender, sexual orientation, or a number of other characteristics. Values of 1 indicate never experiencing a particular form of discrimination, and values of 6 indicate that the respondents perceive themselves as facing this type of mistreatment "almost every day." As with perceptions of major-life racial discrimination, Table 4.2 shows that men, on average, report higher levels of everyday discrimination than do women.

I investigate the relationship between perceptions of everyday discrimination and self-satisfaction in much the same was as I did for Table 4.1, that is, by conducting multivariate ordinal logistic regression models with self-satisfaction as the dependent variable. All of the control variables used in Table 4.1 are also used in Table 4.3: educational attainment, household income, ethnic group, racial ideology, marital status, and gender. Self-satisfaction is again measured on a scale of 1 to 4, with higher values indicating greater *dissatisfaction*.

Table 4.2   Means by Gender, Among Afro-Caribbean and African American Respondents, 2001–2003 *National Survey of American Life (NSAL)*.

	Men	Women
You've been treated with less courtesy than other people.	2.61	2.44
You've been treated with less respect than other people	2.48	2.32
You've received poor service compared with other people at restaurants or stores.	2.33	2.21
People act as if they think you are not smart.	2.60	2.47
People act as if they are afraid of you.	2.39	1.84
People act as if they think you are dishonest.	2.21	1.82
People act as if they are better than you are.	2.98	2.79
You've been called names or insulted.	1.88	1.77
You've been threatened or harassed.	1.63	1.52
You've been followed around in stores.	2.20	2.03

Note: Higher numbers indicate perceiving more frequent experiences with general, everyday discrimination.

Rather than running separate regression models for men and women, the analyses presented in Table 4.3 present a different approach for understanding the complexity of gender. I use an *interaction term* between gender and each of the specific forms of discrimination to show how, in some cases, gender may mediate the relationship between perceptions of discrimination and self-satisfaction.[v] Table 4.3 presents the summary of results from 20 regression models. In models 1 through 10, there are no interaction terms used. The coefficients presented show, first, the relationship between particular forms of everyday discrimination and self-satisfaction and, second, the relationship between gender self-satisfaction, controlling for the other independent variables in the model. In every case, higher scores on perceptions of everyday discrimination are significantly associated with increased risk of greater self-dissatisfaction. Importantly, in each of models 1 through 10, the coefficient for gender is not statistically significant, suggesting that gender plays a limited role in self-satisfaction scores once the other variables in the model are taken into consideration.

---

[v] See Jaccard (2001) for a more thorough explanation of interaction terms in logistic regression models.

Table 4.3   Does Everyday Discrimination Significantly Affect Individuals' Self-Satisfaction? Exponentiated Coefficients from Ordinal Logistic Regression Models, 2001–2003 *National Survey of American Life (NSAL).*

	Models 1–10 (No interaction terms)	Models 11–20 (With Interaction terms)
(1) You've been treated with less courtesy than other people.	1.130 **	1.174***
Gender (Women = 1)	1.078	1.266+
Gender * Courtesy		0.941
(2) You've been treated with less respect than other people.	1.164***	1.237***
Gender (Women = 1)	1.080	1.383*
Gender * Respect		0.907*
(3) You've received poor service compared with other people at restaurants or stores.	1.150***	1.195***
Gender (Women = 1)	1.074	1.242
Gender * Service		0.940
(4) People act as if they think you are not smart.	1.130***	1.080*
Gender (Women = 1)	1.068	0.887
Gender * Not Smart		1.074+
(5) People act as if they are afraid of you.	1.090***	1.164***
Gender (Women = 1)	1.105	1.459**
Gender * Afraid		0.882**
(6) People act as if they think you are dishonest.	1.133***	1.201***
Gender (Women =1)	1.106	1.384**
Gender * Dishonest		0.899*
(7) People act as if they are better than you are.	1.139***	1.146***
Gender (Women = 1)	1.091	1.120
Gender * Better than you		0.991
(8) You've been called names or insulted.	1.154***	1.162***
Gender (Women =1)	1.083	1.108
Gender * Insulted		0.988

(continued)

Table 4.3   (continued)

	Models 1–10 (No interaction terms)	Models 11–20 (With Interaction terms)
(9) You've been threatened or harassed.	1.236***	1.311***
Gender (Women = 1)	1.089	1.283+
Gender * Threaten		0.905
(10) You've been followed around in stores.	1.151***	1.215***
Gender (Women = 1)	1.074	1.306*
Gender * Followed		0.915+

Note: Control variables include gender, ethnic group, generation, household income, educational attainment, racial attitudes, and marital status.
Number of cases range from 4,744 to 4,774.
* significant at 5%; ** significant at 1%; *** significant at 0.1%, with a two-tailed test.
+ Indicates significance only with a one-tailed, directional test (p < 0.05)

Models 11 through 20 are identical to Models 1 through 10, but include an additional interaction term: gender (0 for men and 1 for women) multiplied by respondents' score on particular forms of everyday discrimination. Since men score zero on the interaction term (because their value on gender is zero, and zero multiplied by any score on discrimination will also be zero), the interaction term helps to assess how the relationship between everyday discrimination and self-satisfaction may differ for women and men. Consider, for example, the relationship between being treated disrespectfully and self-satisfaction. The positive coefficient in Model 2 (1.164***) indicates that respondents who report higher frequencies of being treated disrespectfully (higher levels on the independent variable) are more likely to report high levels of self-dissatisfaction (higher levels on the dependent variable), compared with respondents who report lower levels of this mistreatment. The non-significant coefficient for gender (1.080) would lead many to conclude that gender has no generalizable, or statistically significant, effect on self-satisfaction, once the other variables are included.

However, a multiracial feminist approach reveals a different story. The statistically significant interaction term included in Model 12 (0.907*) indicates that the relationship between being treated disrespectfully and self-satisfaction is likely mediated by gender. Because both the interaction term (0.907*) and the gender term (1.383*) are equal to zero for men, the exponentiated coefficient for disrespect (1.237***) indicates the effect of being treated with disrespect on *men's* dissatisfaction. For men, the odds ratio is 1.237 for a one-unit increase in the frequency of being treated with disrespect. For women, however, the odds ratio is 1.122 (= 0.907*1.237) for a one-unit increase in the frequency of being treated with disrespect. In other words, while for both men and women more frequent experiences of being treated with disrespect increase the likelihood of having higher dissatisfaction, the effect of this mistreatment has a larger impact on men's self-satisfaction compared to that of women. The same pattern holds true with everyday discrimination involving perceptions of fear and dishonesty, as well as being "followed around in stores." For both black men and black women, more frequent experiences of people acting "as if they are afraid of you" or "acting as if they think you are dishonest" and being followed around in stores increases the likelihood of high self-dissatisfaction. But these types of everyday discrimination have a larger impact on the likelihood of men's being highly dissatisfied compared to women. The opposite is true for respondents who perceive that people are treating them "as if they are not smart." For both black men and black women, being treated as if one is not smart increases the likelihood of being highly dissatisfied. However, the positive value of this interaction term suggests that this form of everyday discrimination has a larger impact on the likelihood of women's being highly dissatisfied compared to men. More specifically, the odds ratio for men is 1.080 for a one-unit increase in the frequency of being treated as if one is not smart, and the odds ratio for women is 1.160 (=1.080*1.074).

Conclusion

In their review of the academic literature concerning the impact of racial and ethnic discrimination on health and well-being, David R. Williams, Harold W. Neighbors, and James S. Jackson (2003) underscore the importance of *comprehensive* measures of racial discrimination:

> Discrimination is multidimensional, and its assessment should provide comprehensive coverage of all relevant domains. . . . Because these experiences are largely independent of each other, failure to include relevant events understates exposure to discrimination and thus underestimates the association between acute discrimination and health. (p. 202)

While surveys such as the NSAL ask respondents about their experiences with multiple forms of discrimination and discrimination that takes place in multiple domains, a multiracial feminist perspective highlights some important limitations of these surveys. For example, few ask about gendered-racial or sexualized-racial stereotypes that apply predominantly to women. No large-scale survey that I am aware of specifically addresses racial stereotypes of gay, lesbian, or bisexual individuals. Few prod for age-specific experiences beyond those involving school and work. Though multiracial feminist theories suggest that considering multiple specific reference groups is important for understanding the mistreatment of multiply marginalized people (e.g., racial minority women, racial minority individuals who are elderly), most surveys, including the NSAL do not invoke multiple reference groups. Williams and his colleagues (2003, p. 203) write that it is "crucial for measures of stressors [such as discrimination] to provide adequate representation of all of the stressful experiences occurring in individuals' lives," but a multiracial feminist perspective on racial discrimination reveals that some of the most commonly used measures have significant limitations.

Despite these limited measures, a multiracial feminist approach to modeling racial discrimination can bring more nuance to our understanding of racial inequality, especially as it intersects with other social hierarchies. As we saw in the previous chapter, an intersectional approach to survey research encourages researchers to disaggregate measures of sexism because there is good reason to suspect that people in different social locations will experience different forms of sexism. The same holds true when thinking about racial and ethnic discrimination. Statistical models that measure racial discrimination by averaging frequencies or creating an index variable (e.g., Jang, Chiriboga, & Small, 2008) implicitly assume that their measures of discrimination work equally well for all groups; they assume that experiences with discrimination, harassment, and mistreatment all have roughly the same impact and that this impact is similar for all groups of people.

By disaggregating measures of racial discrimination and exploring how they intersect with differences in ethnicity, age, and gender, a multiracial feminist approach makes fewer assumptions of sameness across diverse social groups. As a result, a multiracial feminist approach opens the door for intersectional findings to emerge. In a paper delivered at the United Nations Commission on the Status of Women, Philomena Essed (2001) wrote,

"Although everyday racism has such an informal ring that it may sound as if it concerns relatively harmless and unproblematic events, the psychological distress due to racism on a day-to-day basis can have chronic adverse effects on mental and physical health. Felt persistently, everyday injustices, including gendered racism, are often difficult to pinpoint, and can be therefore hard to counter."

Survey research rooted in multiracial feminism can help to pinpoint, and thus counter, the persistent racism and gendered racism that Essed describes. Not only do men and women of different age groups report different experiences with discrimination, but these experiences relate to self-satisfaction in complex ways. Tables 4.2 and 4.3 suggest that discrimination in the context of education—people treating you as if you are not smart or being discouraged from pursuing further education—is particularly detrimental for African American and Afro-Caribbean women. Mistreatment by the police is similarly detrimental for black men's and black women's self-satisfaction (Table 4.2), but black men are roughly 4 times as likely to experience this as are black women (Figure 4.2). And as Figure 4.3 shows, perceptions of mistreatment by police are also significantly structured by age.

Writing of the limitations of statistical research for understanding race and racism, sociologist Tukufu Zuberi calls for a "critical evaluation of racist structures that encourage pathological interpretations" of racial statistics (2001, p. 134). And while a critical reinterpretation of statistical "evidence" is certainly needed, a multiracial feminist approach takes this idea a step further—pushing us to rethink our basic approach to *doing* statistical research. We must rethink not only how we interpret statistics but also how these statistics are produced. Which information do survey researchers gather, and which information is ignored? Whose experiences does this information reflect, and whose experiences are not represented? How might our analytic techniques obfuscate the experiences of groups who are already marginalized? In the past two chapters, I have described several techniques for bringing a multiracial feminist perspective to studies of gender, racial, and ethnic discrimination. In the next chapter, I show how a multiracial feminist approach can inform survey research on feminism—and womanism.

5

Complicating the General With Narratives of the Particular

Analyzing "Feminism" With a Multiracial Feminist Approach

"Without sustained analysis of the diverse feminisms among women and the conditions that motivate them, theoretical formulations and strategies for change will continue to veer away from historically subordinate groups."

~Beatriz Pesquera and Denise Segura (1993, p. 95)

Introduction

In the previous two chapters I examined the methodological implications of multiracial feminism for understanding discrimination based on race and gender. I used large national surveys that included men and women from diverse racial and ethnic backgrounds to highlight how intersecting

Source: This chapter is a revised version of Catherine E. Harnois's "Generational Differences in Feminist Identities? Exploring Gender-Conscious Identities Among African American Men and Women", *Sociation Today*, 2(2), 2009, with different framing and analysis, but some borrowed paragraphs.

systems of inequality shape individuals' experiences with discrimination. In this chapter, I demonstrate the importance of using an intersectional approach for understanding how people resist subordination and fight for social justice. We have seen that racial minority women's experiences with discrimination and harassment differ from those of white women. The previous chapter highlighted how racism against African Americans is often gendered. It is perhaps not surprising, then, that feminist and antiracist politics may be similarly influenced by race, gender, and other systems of inequality. Multiracial feminist theories are useful for understanding how inequality is maintained; these same theories can help scholars understand how inequality is resisted.

In this chapter, I explore how a methodological approach rooted in multiracial feminist theorizing can bring an added level of nuance to our understanding of contemporary feminist politics. I begin with a brief overview of the findings from existing survey research on contemporary U.S. feminism, particularly as they concern the relationship between *feminist identities*, *gender ideologies*, and *political generations*. I then discuss how multiracial feminist theories can be used to critique the theories and methods driving much of this survey research.

At its core, multiracial feminism highlights the importance of viewing feminism in relation to multiple intersecting systems of inequality (Baca Zinn & Thornton Dill, 1996). Multiracial feminist theories suggest that racial and ethnic differences shape how individuals approach feminism as well as the *feminist identities*—and the broader *gender-conscious identities*—that individuals choose to adopt. I use the term *gender-conscious identities* to acknowledge explicitly the diversity of identities that convey someone's belief in and commitment to gender justice. By using the term *gender-conscious identities* rather than *feminisms*, I mean to signify something that is broader than feminism, and that can include identities (such as *womanist*) that explicitly reject the feminist label. Gender-conscious identities include those identities that speak to individuals' (1) recognition of gender inequality, (2) view of this inequality as problematic, and (3) commitment to social justice and equality more broadly. But they do not necessarily indicate a commitment to gender justice that supersedes other forms of social justice. Analyzing these alternative gender-conscious identities alongside feminist identities can help researchers better understand the relationships among particular feminist identities, as well as the interconnections among multiple systems of inequality. By broadening the types of feminism included in survey research, scholars can gain a more nuanced and inclusive understanding of contemporary feminist politics.

General Narratives of Feminist Identities, Attitudes, and Political Generations

Much of the recent social science research on feminism has been directed at one of two related issues. The first concerns the relationship between gender-related attitudes and feminist identities (e.g., Harnois, 2005; Liss, Hoffner, & Crawford, 2000; Liss, O'Connor, Morosky, & Crawford, 2001; McCabe, 2005; Rhodebeck, 1996; Russo, 1998; Schnittker, Freese, & Powell, 2003), and the second concerns the importance of political generations. Sociologists use the term *political generation* to refer to a group of people who experience shared formative sociopolitical conditions (Mannheim 1952), and political generations are thought to affect both individuals' gender ideologies and their decision to identify as feminist (e.g., Bolzendahl & Myers, 2004; Mann & Huffman, 2004; Peltola et al., 2004; Purvis, 2004; Schnittker et al., 2003; Siegel, 1997; Whittier, 1995).

Scholars seeking to understand generational differences in contemporary feminism have typically framed their analyses around the decline of *second wave* feminism in the early 1980s and the subsequent emergence of *third wave* feminism and *post-feminism* in the mid-1990s.[i] Survey researchers in particular have investigated the extent to which contemporary young women embrace feminist beliefs and identities, and how feminism today compares to that of earlier generations. For example, Huddy and colleagues (2000, p. 311) document widespread support for many dimensions of gender equality, and they show that this support has remained stable since the early 1970s. The authors conclude that support for the women's movement showed "no sign of diminishing in the 1990s" and that "[y]oung people remain staunch movement supporters" (2000, pp. 316–317). In their analysis of feminist attitudes as captured in the 1974 to 1998 General Social Surveys (GSS), Bolzendahl and Myers (2004) similarly document continued support for feminist ideals. Feminist attitudes among women and men, they find, "have continued to liberalize . . . with the exception of abortion attitudes, which have remained stable" (2004, p. 760).

Despite the increasing acceptance of pro-feminist attitudes, survey research indicates that these attitudinal changes have not corresponded with an increase in the number of men and women who describe themselves as feminist. Bivariate analyses from Huddy and colleagues (2000) and Peltola and colleagues (2004) reveal that young women today self-identify

---

[i] See Harnois (2008) and Aronson (2003) for a description of third wave feminism and post-feminism.

as feminist at rates similar to previous generations. However, multivariate models reveal a more complex picture. Analyzing data from the 1992 National Election Study (NES) and the 1996 General Social Survey, Peltola and colleagues conclude that "Baby Bust women [i.e., those born 1960–1978] are less apt to identify as feminist than are older women, once background characteristics and attitudes related to feminist identification are controlled" (2004, p. 122). Similarly, in their multivariate models, Schnittker and colleagues (2003, p. 614) find that "both male and female respondents whose political coming-of-age coincides with the development of the feminist movement are more likely to think of themselves as feminists than are their older or younger counterparts." Taken as a whole, the existing survey research suggests a complex relationship among political generation, gender-related attitudes, and feminist identities. While young people today support feminist aims at rates similar to, or higher than, previous generations, these attitudes appear less likely to translate into feminist identities.

Complicating the General With Multiracial Feminist Theories

Studies that link changes in feminist identities to broader changes in the ideological and political landscapes offer important insights for understanding contemporary feminism. The findings concerning gender-related attitudes underscore the successes of the feminist movement, while the findings concerning feminist identities may suggest some lingering negative connotations attached to the "feminist" label. When viewed from a multiracial feminist perspective, however, an important limitation to this research soon becomes apparent. Namely, in much of the existing survey research on feminism, race is assumed to play a relatively minor role in shaping feminist beliefs and identities.

While survey researchers typically include race (and in some cases ethnicity) among their independent variables, modeling race in this way limits the extent to which they can draw meaningful conclusions about how racial differences shape feminism. For example, in her analysis of data from the 1996 GSS, McCabe (2005) includes race as one of several independent variables and finds that it is not a statistically significant predictor of women's self-identification as feminist. Analyzing the same data, Schnittker and colleagues (2003) found no significant difference among black and white women's feminist identities, but they did find that "other nonwhite women" were more likely than white women to identify as feminist. Peltola and colleagues' (2004) analysis of the 1992 NES and 1996 GSS found more mixed results: Race was a significant predictor of women's feminist identities in the former survey (with white women being less likely than racial-minority women to identify as feminist), but it was non-significant in their analysis of the latter. Taken as a whole, these studies imply that feminist identities among African Americans are shaped by the same processes that influence feminist identities among whites; they suggest that racial statuses play little role in shaping feminist identities.

Situating Feminism Within a Multiracial Feminist Framework

In contrast to much of the existing survey research, multiracial feminist theories suggest that it is important to understand women's relationship with feminism as having potentially as much (or more) to do with race as it does with gender.[ii] Some research has found that racial statuses shape individuals' attitudes about gender (e.g., Blee & Tickamyer, 1995; Cole & Zucker, 2007; Dugger, 1988; Kane, 2000; Ransford & Miller, 1983); and some evidence suggests that racial statuses mediate the relationship between feminist attitudes and feminist identities (Cole & Zucker, 2007; Harnois, 2005). Moreover, multiracial feminist scholarship suggests that race plays an important role in the particular "feminist" identities that individuals choose to adopt (Hill Collins, 1996/2006; hooks, 1984; Phillips, 2006; Walker, 1983/2006). In brief, a multiracial feminist approach challenges the general narrative of feminism described above by suggesting that each aspect of feminism—feminist attitudes, feminist identities, and feminist generations—may be shaped by racial difference and inequality.

For example, in much statistical research, particularly in those studies that use large-scale general surveys, feminist identity is often assessed with a single dichotomous variable, such as "Do you think of yourself as a feminist or not?" (see, for example, Harnois 2008; McCabe 2005; Peltola et al., 2004; Schnittker et al., 2003; Swami & Tovée, 2006).[iii] And while there are exceptions, the "feminist beliefs" explored in this research are generally those associated with liberal feminism. Even when tools that capture the diversity of feminisms are available (e.g., Henley et al.'s 1998 Feminist Perspectives Scale), researchers continue to centralize liberal feminism in their analyses (see, for example, Bay-Cheng & Zucker, 2007; Fingeret & Gleaves, 2004; McCabe, 2005; Schick, Zucker, & Bay-Cheng, 2008).

While survey research on feminism has largely overlooked gender-conscious identities other than feminist, multiracial feminism theorizes these

---

[ii] See Ntiri (2001), who argues that for Africana women, race and class are "superordinate" statuses relative to gender.

[iii] For exception, see Rubin, Nemeroff, and Russo's (2004) study of body consciousness and feminist identity.

alternative identities as critical for understanding racial and ethnic minority women's relationship with feminism. Identities such as black feminist, womanist, and Africana womanist are each thought to invoke a broad commitment to social justice and equality, and a refusal to privilege one dimension of equality over others. Phillips (2006, p. xx), for example, describes womanism as "a social change perspective rooted in Black women's and other women of color's everyday experiences and everyday methods of problem solving . . . extended to the problem of ending all forms of oppression for all people, restoring the balance between people and the environment/nature, reconciling human life with the spiritual dimension." Walker (1983/2006, p. 19) provides multiple approaches for understanding womanism, describing *womanists* as those who are "committed to survival and wholeness of entire people, male *and* female." Hill Collins (2000, p. 43) writes of black feminism that it "requires searching for justice not only for U.S. Black women, but for everyone." And for Hudson-Weems, who coined the term, "Africana womanism," seeks to "enhance future possibilities for the dignity of Africana people and the humanity of all" (1993/2006, p. 53).

Multiracial feminist theories suggest that African American men and women are more likely to embrace these broad gender-conscious identities than they are to embrace the identity of feminist. For a number of reasons—including the history of racial inequality within the women's movement, negative perceptions of feminism within the civil rights movements (see hooks, 1984; Ntiri, 2001; Roth, 2004; Walker, 1983/2006), and media depictions of feminism as a predominantly white women's movement (Hill Collins, 1996/2006)—many African Americans who support gender equality do not describe themselves as feminist. Some multiracial feminist scholars have argued that on its own, the feminist label suggests a commitment to gender justice that is both separate from and more important than one's commitment to other social justice issues. And while there are differences among them, identities such as "womanist," "Africana womanist," and "Black Feminist" each "elevate all sites and forms of oppression . . . to a level of equal concern and action" (Phillips, 2006, pp. xx–xxi). In so far as these identities act as both as race- and gender-conscious identities, they offer an important alternatives for having to choose between privileging either race or gender (see King, 1988).

Related to issues of identity are questions concerning the meaning of feminism itself. Within and outside the academy, *feminism* is a highly contested term; there are many diverse approaches to feminist theory and politics. However, as we saw in Chapter 2, survey research on feminism often centralizes liberal feminism, emphasizing issues such as abortion, equal pay, and women's participation in the public sphere.

Missing from these accounts are concerns that are central to other varieties of feminism (e.g., multiracial feminism, eco-feminism, radical feminism, post-colonial feminism). The feminist *attitudes* included in these studies tend to centralize gender inequality, and perhaps this make sense, as gender inequality is certainly an important feminist issue. But gender inequality is certainly not *the only* feminist issue. If, following Barbara Smith (1980, p. 48), we understand feminism as "the political theory and practice to free *all* women: women of color, working-class women, poor women, physically challenged women, lesbians, old women—as well as white economically privileged heterosexual women," then racial inequality, class inequality, heterosexism, and age inequalities are also important feminist issues. If we expand our understanding of feminism to include post-colonial and eco-feminism, then global capitalism, economic development, sustainability, and climate change are all potential feminist issues as well. This is not to suggest that every analysis of feminism needs to include every potential feminist issue and every variety of feminism. But rather, to the extent that these issues are systematically marginalized or excluded in studies of feminist attitudes, the resulting knowledge claims are limited and also potentially biased.

A third insight offered by multiracial feminist theory concerns the historical narrative of feminism on which most survey research—and a good portion of non-survey research—is based. Social scientists have alternatively described the 1980s as a period of feminist backlash (Faludi, 1992) or "abeyance" (Taylor, Whittier, & Pelak, 2001). And, as mentioned previously, much survey research seems to confirm this, as individuals whose political coming-of-age coincided with this time period are much less likely than individuals in the previous generation to transform their pro-feminist beliefs into feminist identities.

Multiracial feminists have challenged the dominant historical narrative of the women's movement, however, arguing that it better reflects the ebb and flow of white women's feminist activism than it does that of racial- and ethnic-minority women. Roth (2004), for example, argues that what is generally thought of as one single "Second Wave" of American feminism in the 1960s and 1970s in actuality comprised several distinct feminist movements, each with its own origins and time lines: a black feminist movement, a Chicana feminist movement, and a primarily white women's movement. Thompson (2002) further argues that the alleged gap between the "Second Wave" and "Third Wave" of U.S. feminism (i.e., the 1980s) corresponds with a comparatively vibrant period for racial and ethnic minority feminists. Among other things, the 1980s saw the establishment of the National Black Women's Health Project, the founding of Kitchen Table/Women of Color Press, the election of Wilma Mankiller as the first principal chief of the Cherokee Nation, and the publication of many of the most prominent works of multiracial and black feminism (Thompson, 2002). While racially - sensitive narratives of U.S. feminism are emerging from feminist scholarship in the humanities (see, for example, Breines, 2006), disciplinary divides have helped to deter these narratives from crossing over into survey research.

In what follows, I demonstrate a third approach to bridging humanistic theories of multiracial feminism with survey research methods. I consider how our measures and models of feminism might change if researchers centralized the experiences of racial minority women. How do feminist identities differ from other gender-conscious identities, and in what ways are they similar? And to what extent do narratives of general U.S. feminism obscure the diversity of U.S. feminisms and how they relate to one another?

Re-modeling With Multiracial Feminism: Making the Most of Particularistic Surveys

While the previous two chapters used data from large-scale surveys to illustrate the importance of a multiracial feminist framework, this chapter uses a different strategy. The data I analyze come from the 2004 to 2005 National Black Feminist Study (NBFS), a survey designed by political scientist Evelyn Simien. Unlike the surveys analyzed in the previous chapters, this survey was designed specifically to assess feminism and politics within African American communities, and the NBFS was administered only to respondents who describe themselves as African American. In contrast to the GSS and National Survey of American Life (NSAL), which each contain information from several thousand respondents, the sample size of the NBFS is much smaller: a total of 500 respondents.

As described in Chapter 2, small-scale, particularistic surveys, such as the NBFS, offer important benefits for a multiracial feminist approach, but some also contain some important limitations. On the one hand, the lack of racial diversity within the sample limits my ability to investigate racial differences among respondents. Using these data to investigate feminism among African Americans, one loses what McCall (2005) refers to as "intercategorical complexity." It is no longer possible to make direct comparisons across racial groups, since there is only one racial group represented in the sample. On the other hand, because the survey was designed specifically to explore African American politics, analyses of the NBFS have greater potential for revealing more "intracategorical complexity" (McCall, 2005) relative to larger and more general surveys of the U.S. population. While the NBFS contains some questions that are similar to those found in more general surveys (e.g., questions about household income, frequency of church attendance, beliefs about abortion), it also contains a number of questions designed specifically for African American respondents. The NBFS contains a number of questions that assess respondents' beliefs about conditions within black families and churches; it asks respondents about the interconnectedness of race, class, and gender; it also asks respondents if they describe themselves as "feminist," "black feminist," "womanist," or "Africana womanist." Questions such as these can help to illustrate the complexity of feminism within black communities. Moreover, by situating studies of particular feminisms against the backdrop of studies of the general population, we can move beyond "mosaic" or "patchwork quilt" models of difference and begin to understand the relationships that construct these differences. By comparing and contrasting survey research on particular varieties of feminism with research on feminism "in general," we can also see more clearly how general narratives of feminism sometimes misrepresent the beliefs, experiences, and identities of minority groups.

Disaggregating Data to Highlight Difference

The National Black Feminist Study is a valuable source of data for anyone interested in the complexity of contemporary feminism. A national survey drawn from census tracts where at least 30% of the households are African American, the sample consists of 500 adult respondents, all of whom identified as African American.[iv] As previously mentioned, the NBFS is one of the very few surveys to ask respondents about a range of gender-conscious identities, including womanist, Africana womanist, feminist, and black feminist. In addition, the NBFS includes attitudinal measures that speak directly to gender arrangements within the black community and key themes of multiracial feminism. It is thus a valuable resource for understanding how race intersects with gender in the lives of African American women and men.

Despite the clear advantages of this survey, the data set does have some important limitations. As mentioned previously, the respondents are more homogenous with respect to their race, and the sample size is small compared to more general surveys, such as the General Social Survey (GSS) or the National Survey of American Life (NSAL). In the 1996 GSS, for example, 1,381 respondents answered questions concerning their feminist identity (or lack thereof)—in the NBFS, only 487 respondents did. That said, a cursory analysis of the 1996 GSS shows that of those respondents who were asked about their feminist identity, only 168 identified as black or African

---

[iv] Respondents were first asked to identify their racial status. Those who responded "biracial" or "other" were then asked which racial group that they *most* identify with. Respondents who answered African American to either of these questions were included in the sample.

American. With nearly 3 times as many African American respondents answering questions about feminism and with survey questions designed specifically to assess feminism among African Americans, the NBFS may be better suited to understanding African Americans' gender-conscious identities and gender ideologies.

An additional limitation concerns the main variable of interest in this chapter: "Would you describe yourself as a feminist, Black feminist, womanist, Africana womanist, or none of these?" While the diversity of gender-conscious identities included in the question is a key strength of the survey, the phrasing of the question itself may influence how respondents answer. Because the question presents respondents with four different gender-conscious identities from which to choose (in addition to "none of these"), the question itself may prompt respondents to claim an identity, in the context of the survey, that they had not previously held. Despite these limitations, the benefits of a multiracial feminist approach still clearly emerge.

In the analyses that follow, I use two different approaches to explore gender-conscious identities. In my first set of multivariate analyses, I use binary logistic regression models, where respondents who self-identified as "Feminist," "Black Feminist," "Womanist," or "Africana Womanist" are all coded 1 for *holding a gender-conscious identity*. Those who answered *None of these* were coded 0, and respondents who reported *Don't know* or who refused to answer were excluded from the analysis (N = 13). In my second multivariate analysis, I disaggregate these identities by comparing three groups: those who identify as either "Feminist" or "Black Feminist," those who identify as "Womanist" or "Africana Womanist," and those who hold none of these identities. Though there are further distinctions between feminists and black feminists on the one hand and womanists and Africana womanists on the other (Hill Collins, 2000; Hudson-Weems, 2001; Ntiri, 2001), the small number of respondents claiming any one of these particular identities made it difficult to include them separately in the multivariate analyses.

In addition to analyzing the diversity of gender-conscious identities, I examine how these identities relate to political generations and feminist beliefs. Following Peltola and colleagues (2004), I group respondents into three generational cohorts. The "Baby Boom" cohort includes individuals born between 1946 and 1959 (inclusive), the "Pre-Baby Boom" cohort includes those born prior to 1946, and the "Baby Bust" cohort includes those born from 1960 to 1986. Results from previous studies of the general population suggest that women and men of the "Baby Boom" cohort will adopt feminist identities at rates higher than earlier or later generations.

I also examine several variables that assess individuals' *feminist beliefs and attitudes*. So that I can compare my results with those from studies of the general population, I initially focus on attitudes and beliefs that other quantitative studies often include: questions about gender equality and abortion. Specifically, respondents were asked whether they agreed or disagreed that "Black women should share equally in the political leadership of the black community" and that "Black churches or places of worship should allow more black women to become members of the clergy." Responses to each of these variables were coded into four categories, ranging from *strongly disagree* to *strongly agree*. The attitudinal variables were coded from 1 to 4, with higher values reflecting more *feminist responses*. Attitudes toward abortion—another widely used indicator of feminist attitudes—were assessed with the question, "Which of the following best describes your view on abortion? (1) By law, abortion should never be permitted. (2) The law should permit abortion only in cases of rape, incest, or when the life of the women is in danger. (3) The law should permit abortion for reasons other than rape, incest, or danger to the women's life, but only after the need for the abortion has been clearly established. (4) By law, a woman should always be able to obtain an abortion as a matter of personal choice." Higher values on this variable indicate more pro-choice and, arguably, more feminist responses. While the NBFS includes questions that speak more toward multiracial feminism, as opposed to liberal feminism, I begin with these more traditional survey questions to highlight how the narrative of feminism might change by introducing even one theme from multiracial feminism: intersecting identities.

Figure 5.1 shows the frequency distribution of gender-conscious identities for African American men and women. Looking at the left most cluster

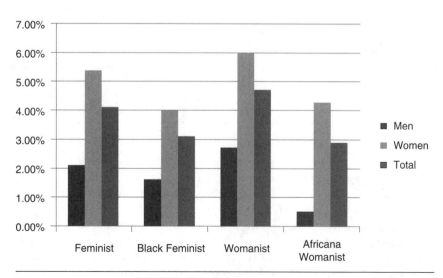

Figure 5.1   Gender-Conscious Identities by Gender

of bars, we see that slightly more than 5% of women and 2% of men report describing themselves simply as "Feminist." For every gender-conscious identity that the survey asks about, the percentage of women who hold that identity is higher than the corresponding percentage of men. This gender difference is expected, and it is consistent with other research on feminist identities. What is perhaps most interesting about this figure, however, is the relationship between feminist identity and gender-conscious identities more generally. The distribution of gender-conscious identities shows that the majority of respondents who hold a gender-conscious identity (72%) identify as something other than simply "Feminist," that is, either "Black Feminist," "Womanist," or "Africana Womanist."[v]

Though the number of respondents who claim any particular gender-conscious identity is small (15% of respondents), Table 5.1 shows that a similar pattern holds true across each political generation.[vi] Within

Table 5.1   African American Men's and Women's Gender-Conscious Identities by Political Generation, 2004–2005 *National Black Feminist Study.*

	Pre-Baby Boom Generation	Baby Boom Generation	Baby Bust Generation
Feminist	1.00%	4.90%	4.80%
	(1)	(7)	(11)
Black Feminist	4.00%	5.60%	0.90%
	(4)	(8)	(2)
Womanist	5.00%	3.50%	5.20%
	(5)	(5)	(12)
Africana Womanist	4.00%	3.50%	2.20%
	(4)	(5)	(5)
None of These	86.00%	82.50%	86.90%
	(86)	(118)	(199)

[v] It is important to note that respondents were presented with a variety of possible gender-conscious identities and then subsequently asked which, if any, they would use to describe themselves. Hearing these options might have influenced which particular gender-conscious identity a respondent chose.

[vi] This general pattern holds true when weights are employed. It also holds when comparing men and women separately. Though the proportion of men who identify as "Womanist" is smaller than the corresponding proportion of women, more than three-quarters of men who embrace a gender-conscious identity identify as something other than simply "Feminist."

each political generation, the percentage of respondents who self-identify as simply "Feminist" is relatively small compared to the percentage of people who hold an alternative gender-conscious identity.

Creating Multiplex Models via Multinomial Logistic Regressions

The simple bivariate analyses presented in the previous table and figure already demonstrate the importance of multiracial feminist theories for understanding and analyzing contemporary feminism. It is clear from these tables that, when given the option to select among multiple gender-conscious identities, African American women and men choose identities other than simply "Feminist." Of those who held gender-conscious identities, fewer than a third identified as "Feminist;" slightly fewer than half identified as either "Feminist" or "Black Feminist."

Beyond emphasizing the existence of diverse gender-conscious identities, multiracial feminism suggests that these identities may develop in qualitatively different ways and that the beliefs associated with particular identities may also differ. To investigate these ideas further, the next portion of my analysis uses multivariate regression models. I begin by exploring some basic sociodemographic predictors of gender-conscious identities and then turn my attention to the beliefs held by feminists, black feminists, womanists, and Africana womanists.

The results from the first set of multivariate regression models are presented in Table 5.2. The dependent variable used in each model is a dichotomous variable, where *holding a gender-conscious identity* is coded 1 and *not holding a gender-conscious identity* is coded 0. Model 1 examines the relationship between gender, gender-related attitudes, and gender-conscious identities. The gender-related attitudes included in this model reflect liberal feminist ideals concerning equality of opportunity and access to abortion. Gender is clearly significant, with women being more than 3 times as likely as men to hold a gender-conscious identity. Interestingly, two of the attitudinal measures are statistically significant, and one is not. Attitudes about abortion and attitudes about gender equality within the political leadership of the black community are significant predictors of gender-conscious identities. Attitudes related to gender equality in black churches, however, do not significantly affect the likelihood of holding a gender-conscious identity.

In the second model, I investigate the relationship between gender-conscious identities, gender, and political generation. As in the first model, gender remains a statistically significant predictor of gender-conscious identities. Controlling for political generation, women are roughly 3 times as

Table 5.2   Odds Ratios From Multivariate Logistic Regression Analyses of Gender-Conscious Identities on Selected Variables, 2004–2005 *National Black Feminist Study.*

	Model 1	Model 2	Model 3	Model 4
Gender (women = 1)	3.123***	3.140***	2.973**	3.186***
	(0.35)	(0.32)	(0.35)	(0.36)
Gender Equality in Black Churches?	1.251	-	1.224	1.254
	(0.15)		(0.15)	(0.15)
Gender Equality in Black Community's Political Leadership?	5.175*	-	5.131*	6.407*
	(0.72)		(0.72)	(0.74)
Women's Legal Right to Abortion?	1.302*	-	1.322*	1.538**
	(0.13)		(0.13)	(0.15)
Generation:				
Baby Boom (1946–1959)		1.412	1.448	1.38
		(0.28)	(0.31)	(0.34)
Education				0.652**
				(0.14)
Marital Status				
Divorced or Separated				0.945
				(0.13)
Single or Cohabiting				0.68
				(0.34)
Religious Service Attendance				0.981
				(0.17)
N	423	472	411	407

Note: Numbers in parentheses are standard errors.
Note: Reference category in the dependent variable is "no gender-conscious identity."
* significant at 5%; ** significant at 1%; *** significant at 0.1% (two-tailed tests)

likely to hold a gender-conscious identity compared with men. Interestingly, however, political generation is not shown to be a statistically significant factor.[vii] This is also the case in Model 3, when gender-related attitudes and political generation are together in the model.

[vii] This is true when the "Baby Boom" generation is included in the model and the earlier and later generations serve together as the reference group, as shown here. Political generation is also non-significant when the earlier and later generations are included in the model individually and when the "Baby Boom" generation is the reference group.

Model 4 represents the full model, which adds controls for a variety of sociodemographic characteristics: marital status, religious service attendance, and educational attainment. Marital status is measured by two variables, "single or cohabiting" and "divorced or separated," where "married or widowed" is the reference category. Religious service attendance is measured with a four-category ordinal-level variable ranging from *never* (coded 1) to *at least once a week* (coded 4). While ideally educational attainment would be measured by a series of dummy variables, here I measure it by using one ordinal-level variable. My decision to do this is based on the relatively small sample size and the small proportion of respondents who claim a gender-conscious identity.

Again, the significant relationships found in Models 1, 2, and 3 remain significant in this model. Women are more than 3 times as likely as men to hold a gender-conscious identity, and attitudes about abortion and gender equality within the black community's political leadership are significant predictors of holding a gender-conscious identity. In addition, it appears that education has a significant effect on gender-conscious identities, but its effect is different from what previous research suggests. When we consider the gender-conscious identities among African American men and women, it appears that increased educational attainment lessens the likelihood of holding a gender-conscious identity. Interestingly, neither marital status nor religious service attendance is significantly associated with holding a gender-conscious identity, once information from variables is taken into consideration. The *lack* of a statistically significant relationship between religiosity and gender-conscious identities stands in contrast to much of the existing survey research on feminism and religiosity in the general population.

In the next portion of my analysis, I disaggregate gender-conscious identities and investigate the extent to which the correlates of feminist and black feminist identities differ from the correlates of womanist and Africana womanist identities. I use the same independent variables as before, but my dependent variable now has three categories: those who hold feminist and black feminist identities, those who hold womanist and Africana womanist identities, and those who hold no gender-conscious identities. Table 5.3 shows the results from the multinomial logistic regression models, where each coefficient describes how the independent variable relates to the named group (i.e., feminists or womanists) compared to the reference group (i.e., those who hold no gender-conscious identity).

Reading down the column for Feminists and Black Feminists, we can see that, compared to men, women are 2.78 times as likely to identify as feminist or black feminist as opposed to holding no gender-conscious identity. In other words, being a woman increases the likelihood of embracing

Table 5.3   Odds Ratios From Multinomial Regression Analysis of Feminist and Womanist Identities on Socio-Demographic and Attitudinal Variables, 2004–2005 *National Black Feminist Study.*

	Feminist or Black Feminist	Womanist or Africana Womanist
Gender (women = 1)	2.785*	3.832**
	(0.49)	(0.51)
Gender Equality in Black Community's Political Leadership?	6.893+	6.047+
	(1.05)	(1.02)
Gender Equality in Black Churches?	1.299	1.201
	(0.22)	(0.20)
Women's Legal Right to Abortion?	1.604*	1.489*
	(0.20)	(0.20)
Generation:		
Baby Boom (1946–1959)	2.320+	0.780
	(0.45)	(0.48)
Education	0.442***	0.872
	(0.22)	(0.17)
Marital Status		
Divorced or Separated	0.933	0.938
	(0.17)	(0.17)
Single or Cohabiting	0.773	0.639
	(0.48)	(0.44)
Religious Attendance	0.964	1.068
	(0.24)	(0.21)
N		407

Note: Reference category in the dependent variable is "no gender-conscious identity." Numbers in parentheses are standard errors.
* significant at 5%; ** significant at 1%; *** significant at 0.1% (two-tailed tests).
+ significant at 5%, one-tailed test.

a feminist or black feminist identity, as opposed to holding no gender-conscious identity. In addition, beliefs about abortion and gender equality in the leadership of the black community are similarly powerful predictors of gender-conscious identities. Those who believe strongly in gender equality in political leadership are much more likely to hold a feminist identity, as opposed to claiming no gender-conscious identity. Each unit increase in agreement (e.g., a move from *agree* to *strongly agree*) increases the likelihood of holding a feminist identity nearly sixfold.

Two sociodemographic characteristics also help distinguish feminists and black feminists from those who hold no gender-conscious identities. Being a member of the baby boom generation more than doubles the likelihood that African American men and women will embrace a feminist identity (as opposed to holding no gender-conscious identity). Educational attainment is shown to be negatively associated with the likelihood of adopting a feminist or black feminist identity. The odds ratio of less than 1.0 indicates that those with greater educational attainment are less likely to embrace a feminist identity than those with lower educational attainment. The generational differences found in this model are supported by much of the existing research on feminist identities in the general population. However, the negative effect of educational attainment, as well as the non-significance of religious service attendance, challenge much of the dominant thinking concerning the correlates of feminist identities.

The right half of the table describes how individuals who hold womanist and Africana womanist identities differ from those who hold no gender-conscious identities. When comparing the predictors of feminist identities with those of womanist identities, several important findings emerge. First, gender is again shown to be a powerful predictor of self-identification as womanist or Africana womanist. Compared to men, women are more than 3 times as likely to identify as a womanist, as opposed to holding no gender-conscious identity. Second, attitudes about abortion are again shown to be an important predictor of gender-conscious identities. African Americans who support abortion rights are more likely to identify as womanists or Africana womanists, as opposed to claiming no gender-conscious identity. A third important feature of Table 5.3 concerns the absence of generational differences in womanist identities. While membership in the baby boom generation increases the likelihood that individuals adopt feminist or black feminist identities, as opposed to holding no gender-conscious identity, generational differences do not predict womanist identities in the same way. There appear to be no significant generational differences in womanist identities, once attitudes and sociodemographic factors are taken into consideration. The same is true for educational attainment. While increased educational attainment decreases the likelihood that an African American individual adopts a feminist or black feminist identity, as opposed to claiming no gender-conscious identity, educational attainment does not help predict who claims a womanist identity.

On the whole, the results from these analyses underscore the importance of considering multiple gender-conscious identities when assessing feminism among African Americans. African Americans clearly embrace a variety of gender-conscious identities, and it appears that the particular identities of "Feminist or Black Feminist" and "Womanist or Africana Womanist" may

Table 5.4   Percentage of Respondents Who Strongly or Somewhat Agree With the Key Themes of Multiracial Feminism, 2004–2005 *National Black Feminist Study.*

	Feminists	Womanists	No G-C I*
The problems of racism, poverty, and sexual discrimination are linked.	72.73	89.19	75.31
Black women have suffered from both sexism and racism.	73.53	81.25	81.91
Black feminist groups should advance position of black women.	84.38	82.35	76.55

Note: *Gender-Conscious Identities.

be shaped by different social processes. While the dominant narrative of feminist waves and political generations appears to be somewhat useful in predicting African Americans' feminist identities, political generations may not shape womanist identities in the same way.

While the regression models presented above suggest that attitudes about political leadership and abortion are significantly related to African Americans' womanist and feminist identities, any analysis of black feminism and womanism would be remiss if it examined only liberal feminist attitudes. The last portion of my analysis, therefore, investigates how gender-conscious identities intersect with multiracial feminist beliefs. Table 5.4 presents the percentages of Feminists and Black Feminists, Womanists and Africana Womanists, and those who hold no gender-conscious identity who agree with three central claims of multiracial feminism: the intersection of race, class, and gender; the simultaneity of oppression; and the importance of black feminist activism. The vast majority of respondents agree with the claims of multiracial feminism, and this is true regardless of respondents' gender-conscious identity or lack thereof.

Table 5.5 takes this analysis a step further, investigating whether gender-conscious identities correlate with multiracial feminist beliefs, controlling for gender and generation. In this table, each model investigates the extent to which gender-conscious identity, gender, and generation predict one theme of multiracial feminist theory. The first explores how identity, generation, and gender relate to beliefs about the linkages among race, class, and gender; the second concerns how these factors relate to individuals' beliefs about sexism and racism in the lives of black women; and the third explores how identity, generation, and gender correlate with perceptions of black feminism.

Looking across the table, we can see that gender-conscious identities are significant predictors of respondents' beliefs about two of the three themes.

Table 5.5   Odds Ratios From Ordinal Logistic Regression Models of Multiracial Feminist Beliefs on Selected Variables, 2004–2005 *National Black Feminist Study.*

	(1) The problems of racism, poverty, and sexual discrimination are linked	(2) Black women have suffered from both sexism and racism	(3) Black feminist groups should advance position of black women
Gender-Conscious Identity:			
Feminist or Black Feminist	0.905	0.845	2.368*
	(0.37)	(0.35)	(0.39)
Womanist or Africana Womanist	3.736**	1.127	1.387
	(0.46)	(0.37)	(0.35)
Generation:			
Baby Boom (1946–1959)	1.573*	1.122	0.916
	(0.21)	(0.20)	(0.20)
Gender (Women = 1)	0.649*	0.845	0.656*
	(0.20)	(0.19)	(0.19)
N	456	439	424

Note: Numbers in parentheses are standard errors.
* significant at 5%; ** significant at 1%; *** significant at 0.1% (two-tailed tests)

Compared to those who hold no gender-conscious identity, those who identify as womanist or Africana womanist are more likely to agree that the problems of racism, poverty, and sexual discrimination are linked. The non-significance of the coefficient for feminists and black feminists suggests that, controlling for gender and generation, this group does not significantly differ in their agreement from those who hold no gender-conscious identity. On the other hand, Model 3 suggests that those who identify as feminist or black feminist are significantly more supportive of black feminist groups than those who hold no gender-conscious identity. This is not necessarily surprising, given that people who identify as feminists or black feminists probably hold black feminism in high regard. Finally, there is some support for political generation affecting respondents' support for multiracial feminist ideals. Political generation is not a significant predictor in Models 2 and 3, but Model 1 suggests that individuals in the baby boom generation are more likely to view racism, poverty, and sexual discrimination as interconnected, compared with older and younger generations.

Situating the Particular Within the General to Highlight Relationality

Taken as a whole, the above analyses help illustrate the importance of a multiracial feminist, or intersectional, approach for understanding and analyzing contemporary feminism. I argued at the beginning of this chapter that humanistic theories of multiracial feminism offered important challenges for general survey research on feminism. In particular, multiracial feminism highlights the need to understand feminist attitudes, identities, and generations within a broader context of intersecting systems of inequality. Collectively, the analyses presented in this chapter illustrate the advantages of a multiracial feminist approach. First, it is clear from Figure 5.1 that, when given the option to select among multiple gender-conscious identities, African American women and men frequently choose identities other than simply "Feminist." Of those who held gender-conscious identities, less than a third identified as "Feminist;" slightly less than half identified as either "Feminist" or "Black Feminist." Given the variety of gender-conscious identities that African American women and men appear to hold, the survey question, "Do you think of yourself as a feminist or not?" (which regularly appears in surveys of the general population) seems a poor measure of gender-conscious identities among African Americans. The extent to which this measurement bias has affected the findings of previous research is unclear, but it likely has helped to obfuscate racial differences in feminist identities.

Despite the diversity of gender-conscious identities among African Americans, the results from Table 5.3 suggest that political generations do play a role in shaping the gender-conscious identities of African Americans. Membership in the baby boom generation increases the likelihood of individuals' adopting a feminist or black feminist identity, as opposed to holding no gender-conscious identity. As shown in Table 5.5, political generation also appears to play some role in shaping respondents' support for multiracial feminist ideals.

In addition to complicating the relationship between political generations and gender-conscious identities, a multiracial feminist approach sheds light on the meanings associated with feminist and womanist identities. The analyses presented here, in particular the disaggregated analysis of gender-conscious identities, reveal important insights concerning the meaning of particular gender-conscious identities as well as the contexts in which they are likely to develop. First, while some previous research suggests that increased education and decreased religiosity both increase the likelihood of holding a feminist identity (e.g., Peltola et al., 2004) a multiracial feminist approach yields a more complex picture. As shown in Tables 5.2 and 5.3, religious service attendance is not a significant predictor of gender-conscious identities among African Americans. And, while educational attainment *is* a statistically significant predictor of gender-conscious identities in general and feminist identities in particular, its effect is opposite to what is found in many studies of the general population.

Attitudes related to gender arrangements in the black community's political leadership and attitudes about women's legal rights to abortion are consistently strong predictors of African American women's gender-conscious identities—both feminist and womanist. However, controlling for other factors, attitudes about gender arrangements within black churches do not significantly affect the likelihood of African Americans' adopting a gender-conscious identity.

King's (1988) discussion of multiple jeopardies and black feminist consciousness can help shed light on many of these apparent contradictions. She writes that "the conditions that bring black women to feminist consciousness are specific to our social and historical experiences" and that "[m]any of the conditions that middle-class white feminists have found oppressive are perceived as privileges by black women, especially those with low incomes" (1988, p. 71). While feminists have critiqued some religious institutions for perpetuating and justifying gender inequality, many of these same institutions have been important sites of empowerment for African American women (Hill Collins, 1991, 2000; Kane, 2000). If African American women already occupy positions of leadership and power within the church, as suggested by some multiracial feminist theorists, then this helps explain why feelings about gender arrangements within black churches might be unrelated to gender-conscious identities. In addition, if churches have historically been sites of resistance against a racist society (Hill Collins, 2000; hooks, 1984; Kane, 2000) and African American women have had to negotiate their fight for gender equality in such a way as to minimize the hurt done to or the blame assigned to their "comrades in struggle," that is, African American men (hooks, 1984; see also Crenshaw, 1991; King, 1988), then this helps explain why gender-conscious identities may have more to do with beliefs about politics rather than beliefs about church.

Conclusion

Philosopher Elizabeth Spelman introduces her book *Inessential Woman: Problems of Exclusion in Feminist Thought* by explaining that for feminism, the "problem" of diversity as conventionally described "has been how we weigh what we have in common [as women] against what differentiates us." "But the real problem," she explains, "has been how feminist theory has *confused the condition of one group of women with the condition of all*" (1988, p. 4; italics added for emphasis). Surveys designed with a focus on the particular, such as the NSBA, combined with a methodological approach grounded in multiracial feminism, can help elucidate exactly this type of confusion. The narratives of feminism gleaned from studies of the general population present, as one might expect, general narratives. But as Beatriz Pesquera and Denise Segura write in the quotation that opens this chapter, "without sustained analysis of the diverse feminisms among women and the conditions that motivate them, theoretical formulations and strategies for change will continue to veer away from historically subordinate groups" (1993, p. 95). Focusing on the particularity, highlighting intracategorical complexity, and laying the foundation for comparative research, a multiracial feminist approach yields a different and important alternative narrative.

In this and the previous two chapters, I demonstrated three specific approaches for bringing a multiracial feminist approach to social science survey research on sexism, racism, and feminism. In the concluding chapter, I bring together the methodological findings from the previous chapters and outline six considerations for bringing an intersectional approach to survey research.

6

Multiracial Feminism and Survey Research

Re-thinking the "Impossibility of Coherence"

"Because intersectionality requires a both/and way of knowing and a degree of open-mindedness toward ambiguity, women's studies methods do not necessarily seek to smooth over or eradicate paradoxes and differences, but find them to be spaces from within which to work."

~Vivian May (2002, p. 151)

Introduction

In the previous chapters, I argued that multiracial feminist theory offers an important yet underutilized perspective for social science survey research. I critically examined survey research on sex discrimination and harassment, racial discrimination, and feminism and demonstrated how a multiracial feminist approach could inform survey research on each of these issues. I suggested that multiracial feminist theory could contribute to several different types of survey research, ranging from large-scale general surveys to small-scale surveys rooted in the particular.

In this chapter, I bring together the methodological findings from the previous chapters and outline six considerations for bringing an intersectional approach to survey research. Such an approach requires researchers to re-think survey design, measures, and modeling techniques with an eye toward balancing the general and particular. In addition, a multiracial feminist approach requires moving beyond individual-level analyses, and instead viewing race and gender as interacting with other social institutions and as dynamic social institutions in and of themselves. Finally, fully adopting a multiracial feminist approach requires survey researchers to critically re-examine the goals of survey research projects and to expand the theories used to guide this research. Such an approach is useful not only for research on racism, sexism, and feminism, but also for a wide range of survey research, and for social science more generally.

In the opening chapter, I described several key themes of multiracial feminist theorizing. Multiracial feminist theorists have argued that the social world is organized by multiple systems of inequality and that these systems of inequality interact with one another in complex and dynamic ways. Systems of race, gender, class, and sexuality intersect at the individual level, the institutional level, and every level in between. It is not simply that multiply marginalized individuals experience multiple forms of discrimination (e.g., racial discrimination, gender discrimination, and class-based discrimination). Nor is it simply that multiply marginalized individuals experience discrimination based on multiply marginalized statuses (e.g., racialized gender-discrimination and gendered class–discrimination). Rather, socially-constructed notions of race, class, gender, sexuality, age, physical ability, and ethnicity are both built into and maintained by our political, economic, and cultural institutions (Glenn, 2002; Omi & Winant, 1994; Thornton Dill, 1988; Weber, 2001).

In addition to emphasizing the intersections of systems of inequality (i.e., intersectionality), multiracial feminists have emphasized the agency of marginalized individuals and groups, as well as the "relational nature of dominance and subordination." As Elsa Barkley Brown writes of historical scholarship, "[t]he overwhelming tendency now . . . is to acknowledge and then ignore differences among women" (1992, p. 300). She states,

> We are likely to acknowledge that white middle-class women have had a different experience from African American, Latina, Asian American and Native American women; but the relation, the fact that these histories exist simultaneously, in dialogue with each other, is seldom apparent in the studies we do, not even in those studies that perceive themselves as dealing with the diverse experiences of women. (1992, p. 300)

Multiracial feminist theorizing encourages scholars to move beyond "mosaic" and "patchwork quilt" models of difference by "theorizing difference" (Baca Zinn & Thornton Dill, 1996) within the context of relationships structured by systems of inequality.

Finally, for Baca Zinn and Thornton Dill (1996) and other scholars, multiracial feminist scholarship is distinguished by "wide-ranging methodological approaches" and a commitment to interdisciplinarity. As Berger and Guidroz (2009, p. 7) explain, an intersectional approach encourages "border-crossing" and "challenges traditional ways of framing research inquiries, questions, and methods." In so doing, a multiracial feminist scholarship asks scholars to hold themselves accountable to something beyond traditional disciplinary expectations.

Multiracial Feminism and Survey Research: Suggestions for Moving Forward

Taken together, the key themes of multiracial feminist theory emphasize the importance of recognizing and "dealing effectively" with complex and dynamic systems of difference and inequality. As Lorde (1984, p. 122) wrote of the feminist movement, our reluctance to recognize differences among women and to "deal effectively with the distortions which have resulted from the ignoring and misnaming of those differences" ultimately increases tensions and separation between privileged and underprivileged women. While some feminist scholars initially saw multiracial feminists' emphasis on difference as a threat to solidarity among women (see, for example, Okin, 1999; Young, 2004) and hence a threat to feminism itself, many feminists now see intersectionality as one of the key intellectual contributions of contemporary feminism (Berger & Radeloff, 2011). It may be that the instability emphasized in multiracial feminism—the "impossibility of coherence," the need to continually reconsider and reassess—is among the most important "animating features" of contemporary feminist scholarship (Wiegman, 2002, p. 170).

Within the social sciences today, quantitative survey research and multiracial feminist theory exist in relation to one another in much the same way as early articulations of liberal, women-based feminism and multiracial feminism. That is, the two are frequently viewed as being at odds with one another. Multiracial feminism's emphasis on difference stands in opposition to some of the most foundational elements of quantitative survey research. How, for example, can a series of separate, discrete variables representing individuals' race, gender, and class statuses effectively represent the dynamic, intersecting, and multilevel systems of inequality theorized by multiracial feminists? For survey researchers and proponents of multiracial feminism alike, the tension between the two approaches often results in scholars' dismissing one another's work, rather than creatively engaging with it. Alice Ludvig (2006, p. 246) writes of intersectionality, "[I]ts implications for empirical analysis are, on the one hand, a seemingly insurmountable complexity and, on the other, a fixed notion of differences. This is because the list of differences is endless or even seemingly indefinite. It is impossible to take into account all the differences that are significant at any given moment." For some, the "complexity of intersectionality" leads to a rejection of quantitative analyses; for others, the very same complexity leads to a rejection of multiracial feminism.

But what if, as Wiegman suggests, we reconceived of the tension between the two approaches as a source of intellectual inspiration, that is, as an opportunity to rethink our approach to survey research and feminist scholarship more broadly? As the previous chapters demonstrate, a multiracial feminist perspective sheds light on important limitations of existing survey research on racism, sexism, and feminism. In particular, it reveals the tendency for social science researchers to rely on simplistic measures, rely on homogenous samples, and overlook issues of relationality. It also clarifies the difficulties of drawing meaningful conclusions based on this research. For example, what can we really say about the relationship between race and feminism if, in our surveys, we researchers have overlooked the feminist identities that African American women are most likely to claim? How might our conclusions about feminist attitudes change if, in our research design, we included *both* a diverse sample *and* a broad spectrum of feminist attitudes?

Taken together, the insights of multiracial feminist theory offer new approaches for both viewing (i.e., critiquing) and doing (i.e., producing) feminist survey research. The point is not that multiracial feminism offers some new statistical procedure or new technique to reduce sampling bias, but rather, by deliberately rooting our methodology within multiracial feminism, we open the possibility for an alternative type of research project to emerge. And while there are undoubtedly many different models of multiracial feminist survey research, I want to conclude by offering six suggestions for critiquing and producing survey research from a multiracial feminist perspective. I offer these not as a standard for judging how feminist any given research project is. Rather, these suggestions are meant to prime the minds and imaginations of researchers interested in bringing an intersectional approach to survey research.

Evaluating Measures: How Can Multiracial Feminism Help Us Better Understand Existing Measures?

One of the main benefits of bringing a multiracial feminist perspective to social science survey research is that it can reveal important limitations to existing survey questions and the measures of social phenomena based on them. In particular, a multiracial feminist perspective highlights how our measures are often constructed with an eye toward the experiences of particular groups. Often, our measures work best for groups that are more privileged; they obscure the experiences of those who are already marginalized. For example, survey questions concerning social inequality and discrimination tend to focus on one dimension of inequality, or on one social status, and neglect to consider how other systems of inequality intersect with the dimension that is their focus.[i] Commonly used measures of feminism, for example, highlight the differences between men and women, and commonly used measures of racial discrimination highlight the differences between whites and racial minorities. But as we have seen, measures of feminism often neglect differences of race, class, and sexuality, and measures of racial discrimination often gloss over differences of gender and sexuality.

Survey research that is based on measures that do not capture the lived experiences of diverse social groups is simply not well positioned to reveal the "complexity of intersectionality." But perhaps even more problematically, survey research that aims to make general claims, but that bases these claims on measures that systematically privilege one group over others, can yield misleading conclusions. Recall, for example, how gender-aggregated analyses of racial discrimination obscure both men's and women's experiences with racial discrimination. From the perspective of multiracial feminism, theoretical frameworks that privilege *a priori* one dimension of difference or inequality over others, while neglecting the ways in which this dimension may intersect with other systems of inequality, misrepresent the experiences of individuals who are multiply marginalized. In the context of survey research, this misrepresentation of experience can lead to systematic measurement error, biased findings, and faulty conclusions. In this respect, perhaps the most important analytic intervention that multiracial feminism offers is a theoretical framework for evaluating existing measures.

Social scientists use the term *content validity* to describe the degree to which measures "capture all dimensions or features of the concept as it is

---

[i] In broad terms, Purdie-Vaughns and Eibach (2008) refer to this phenomenon as "intersectional invisibility." See also Cohen (1997) and Crenshaw (1991) for how this phenomenon plays out in public rhetoric and policy.

defined" (Lewis-Beck, Bryman, & Liao, 2004, p. 163). And while there is no quantifiable test of content validity, a good starting point for assessing content validity as it relates to intersecting social statuses is to produce a series of bivariate tables, or crosstabs. Examining how different groups score on particular measures can help to shed light on differences and similarities in the experiences of diverse groups. Comparing Afro-Caribbean men's experiences with discrimination to those of African American men's experiences, we may see a high degree of similarity. But when we compare men's experiences with women, we may see many differences. And while these differences by themselves do not necessarily reflect a low level of content validity, they provide the opportunity for a critical consideration of intersectional differences.[ii] Why are there no forms of racial discrimination included in the NSAL that women report experiencing with greater frequency than men? Does this reflect real-world underlying differences in the amount of racial discrimination experienced by black men and black women? Does it reflect gender differences in *perceptions* of discrimination? Or perhaps, rather than reflecting real-world differences, the gender differences reflect measures of discrimination that are themselves biased—measures that more fully reflect men's experiences with discrimination as compared to women's. It is likely that some combination of these explanations is at work, but the point remains Without a multiracial feminist framework, we are unlikely to determine the extent to which these differences reflect real-world experiences and perceptions, and the extent to which they are a product of our measures.

Designing Surveys: How Can We Balance the General and the Particular?

In addition to providing a framework for critiquing existing survey questions, multiracial feminist theory provides a framework for developing *original survey tools*. As a methodological framework, multiracial feminism emphasizes the value of searching for commonalities and differences, as well as the relationships that structure these differences. At its best, an intersectional framework can shed light on both "intercategorical" and "intracategorical complexity" (McCall, 2005). Survey researchers are best

---

[ii] It is important to note that the presence or absence of differences does not directly speak to the degree of validity. For example, a crosstab may reveal no significant differences across groups, but groups may be interpreting the question in different ways. Alternatively, the crosstab may reveal differences that reflect different life experiences, which does not necessarily reflect low content validity.

able to do this, however, if they have instruments available to them that balance the general and the particular.

There are at least two straightforward strategies for managing this balancing act in survey design. The first is using *skip patterns* within a single survey instrument to direct individuals and groups to questions specifically designed for them. Skip patterns are commonly used in survey design and easily allow a single survey instrument to include both general and specific questions. For example, surveys designed to assess the prevalence of gender discrimination and harassment might include a series of general questions concerning discrimination in the public sphere (e.g., passing remarks, overheard jokes, and the like) and then include a series of questions designed for particular groups, asked only of those respondents who are members of those groups. For example, respondents who are currently working in the paid labor force might be asked one set of questions about discrimination and harassment at work; respondents who are currently enrolled in school might be asked a different set of questions concerning their experiences there; and respondents who are both students *and* workers could be asked *both* sets of questions. A multiracial feminist approach requires examining the intersections of multiple social statuses, and it is possible that attention to a large number of differences simultaneously could feel overwhelming. On the other hand, increasingly sophisticated computing technology makes incorporating and analyzing complicated skip patterns relatively easy.

For small-scale survey research rooted in the particular, skip patterns may be too cumbersome, and, if the sample is intentionally homogenous, skip patterns may be unnecessary. An alternative strategy for balancing the general and the particular in this type of research is to develop *survey questions designed specifically* for the target population and to situate the analyses of *the particular within a broader social context* via theoretical and comparative work. Simien's *National Black Feminist Study (NBFS)* is a great example of this kind of survey instrument. Because the target sample is African Americans, her survey includes a number of questions designed specifically to assess respondents' beliefs about black feminism, feelings about gender arrangements in black churches and families, and feelings about politics within the black community. But while it includes multiple nuanced survey questions concerning the experiences, identities, and attitudes of African Americans, on its own, the NBFS is somewhat limited in its ability to capture how race works in the lives of African Americans. The reason for this, of course, is that by looking exclusively at African Americans' beliefs, experiences, and identities, we are unable to assess directly how these differ from those of other racial and ethnic groups. We may gain a clear view of particularity, but the relationships that structure and help give meaning to particularities and differences remain hidden. By situating the research findings within a broader context and by comparing their findings with those from more general studies, researchers are in a better position to understand both the general and particular.

Both of these strategies equip researchers with what psychologist Nancy Felipe Russo (1998, p. 315) has termed a *double lens* for survey research. Russo, who was concerned with generational differences in feminist attitudes, argued that future surveys of feminist attitudes should employ a "double lens" to better capture generational differences, "one for seeing how far we have come and the other for how far we have yet to go." It is useful to ask seemingly out-of-date survey questions year after year, she suggested, because doing so allows us to document the success of the feminist movement. At the same time, however, we must constantly revise our measures so that they reflect contemporary lived experiences. Many of the forms of racism and sexism that people encounter today are different from what they were two decades ago. Moreover, people struggle to resist subordination, objectification, and oppression more generally, in different ways (consider, for example, how the Internet has changed politics and activism). We need survey instruments that reflect these changes but that retain continuity with previous research. In the same way, we need survey instruments that reflect the diversity of lived experiences while maintaining an ability to reveal commonalities and general patterns.

Constructing Multiplex Models: How Can We Construct Models That Convey Multiple and Diverse Stories?

Many people who would like to do survey research informed by a multiracial feminist perspective are not in a position to create and administer their own surveys. Designing and administering surveys is expensive, especially when administered to large and diverse samples, and space for questions is often at a premium. Fortunately, the insights of multiracial feminism are not limited to survey design; a multiracial feminist approach can also help us to rethink the ways in which we analyze existing survey data. Beyond cross-tabs and other descriptive statistics, multiracial feminist analyses of existing survey data can take a number of different forms. And in some ways, the choice of the most appropriate approach depends on the kind of data that one is analyzing. In each of the previous three chapters, I used a multiracial feminist perspective to inform my analysis. And while each of the chapters relies on a combination of descriptive statistics and regression analyses, the analytic interventions of multiracial feminism differ in each.[iii]

[iii] See also Harnois (2005) and Harnois and Ifatunji (2011), where structural equation modeling is used to bridge multiracial feminist theory and survey research.

In my analysis of workplace sexism (Chapter 3), I analyzed data from a large-scale general survey, which contained relatively few measures of discrimination and harassment, but offered the benefit of a large and diverse national survey. A multiracial feminist perspective pushed me to think about the differences between sexual harassment and gender discrimination at work, which in turn led me to disaggregate what, in much of the existing research, is combined. I explored perceptions of workplace sexual harassment and perceptions of workplace gender discrimination in separate regression models, making fewer assumptions about the similarities between the two. In addition, a multiracial feminist approach pushed me to consider additional forms of workplace discrimination and harassment, and how these intersect with gender discrimination and sexual harassment. Disaggregating the dependent variables and running separate regression analyses for each one, I was able to conclude that different groups of women do appear to face different obstacles at work—and that, in addition to gender, these obstacles are structured by age, racial and ethnic inequalities, and women's marital status.

My analysis of racial and ethnic discrimination employed a different type of survey—one that was designed specifically to assess the experiences of a particular group, African Americans, and that contained multiple specific questions about individuals' perceptions of their own mistreatment. I was interested in how instances of racial and ethnic discrimination affected individual well-being. Multiracial feminist theory suggests that individuals experience different kinds of discrimination, depending on their location within the intersecting hierarchies of gender, race, ethnicity, age, sexuality, and class. Moreover, multiracial feminism suggests that people in different social locations often respond to the world in qualitatively different ways.

In this case too, a multiracial feminist approach pushed me to disaggregate what others have often combined. But whereas in Chapter 3 I disaggregated the *dependent* variable, in Chapter 4, I disaggregated information concerning the *independent* variables. And I did this in several ways. First, rather than creating an index variable about experiences with discrimination, I examined perceptions of each type of discrimination separately. Then, using basic bivariate descriptive statistics, I examined ethnic, gender, and age differences in who was likely to perceive experiencing each type of discrimination. After seeing significant differences in perceptions of discrimination, I then examined the relationship between particular forms of discrimination and individual well-being. In my analysis of the impact of "major-life" racial and ethnic discrimination on individual well-being, I conducted several series of regression analyses, one of which included only men respondents and one of which included only women. While some forms of major-life racial and ethnic discrimination had significant effects on both men's and women's self-satisfaction, some forms of discrimination had seemingly disparate impacts on men's and women's self-satisfaction. My analysis of everyday discrimination employed still a different technique to highlight the intersectionality. Rather than conducting separate regression analyses for men and women, I employed a series of interaction terms to show how the relationship between everyday discrimination and individual well-being is structured by gender. By disaggregating data on discrimination (that is, by examining the impact of particular forms of everyday discrimination rather than employing a composite measure or index variable) and by creating interaction terms between gender and perceptions of each type of discrimination, I was able to highlight the disparate impacts of everyday discrimination on men's and women's well-being.

My analysis of feminism and womanism employed a much smaller survey and a more homogenous sample, and consequently, it employed still a different approach to incorporating a multiracial feminist perspective. The particularity of the NBFS survey questions and sample make it a valuable source for analyzing the richness and nuances of contemporary black feminism and womanism. However, the specificity simultaneously makes it difficult to capture what McCall (2005, p. 1773) refers to as "intercategorical complexity." The NBFS data underscore the complexity of black feminism, but because these data contain information only from respondents who identify primarily as black or African American, scholars analyzing this survey lose the ability to make direct comparisons across racial groups. In this case, a multiracial feminist approach to survey research still emphasized difference, but in order to highlight relationality and the meanings associated with these differences, it was necessary to situate this particular analysis within the broader framework of survey research on feminism in general. By comparing the previous findings of research on seemingly "racially neutral" feminism with my own analysis of black feminism and womanism, a multiracial feminist approach made it possible to clarify the meanings associated with black feminism and womanism while simultaneously highlighting the limitations of general narratives of feminism.

Though the analytic interventions of multiracial feminism differ, in each chapter a multiracial feminist perspective leads to what I refer to as a *multiplex modeling*—statistical modeling that simultaneously conveys multiple and diverse narratives. In taking this approach, I have explicitly rejected the goal of parsimony; the aim is not to develop a general model of perceptions of discrimination or feminist identity development. Rather, the aim is to develop a model or, rather, a series of models that take into consideration the key methodological themes of multiracial feminist theory: difference, simultaneity, intersectionality, relationality. There already exists a range of statistical tools available to analyze survey research in this way, but without a methodological approach rooted in multiracial feminism, it is easy to take general models at face value—as general narratives of the social world—and to overlook the ways in which they may mask differences and inequalities.

Moving Beyond Essentialist Interpretations: How Can We Employ Dummy Variables While Simultaneously Refusing Essentialism?

As mentioned in the introductory chapter, one of the most important feminist critiques of survey research concerns how gender is understood within the context of surveys and statistical analyses. In what has become known as the *gender as a variable* approach, gender is reduced to a single dummy variable and is, essentially, reduced to "sex." While multiracial feminist theorists understand gender as a dynamic system of inequality, operating at multiple levels and interacting with other systems of inequality, survey researchers often gloss over this complexity. Attention is focused on the statistically significant effect (or lack thereof) of gender and is often drawn away from the processes through which gender differences are created.

Fortunately, survey researchers need not confine their understanding of gender to a single dummy variable, and dummy variables need not be interpreted in essentialistic ways. It is possible, as McCall (2005, p. 1773) explains, to "provisionally adopt existing analytic categories to document relationships of inequality among social groups and changing configurations of inequality along multiple and conflicting dimensions." For example, exploring men's and women's experiences with racial discrimination by means of a dummy variable and in conjunction with interaction terms and multiplex models makes no assumption of essential gender differences. Nor does this approach intrinsically understand gender as exclusively a property of individuals. When rooted in a multiracial feminist framework, the dummy variable of gender can highlight interactional and institutional dimensions of gender, as well as show how gender intersects with other systems of inequality. In Chapter 4, employing gender as a dummy variable revealed large gender discrepancies in perceptions of discrimination, as well as significant differences in how particular forms of discrimination affect well-being. While it is possible to interpret these findings in an individualistic, essentialist way, (e.g., men experience more discrimination than women, or males are more likely to perceive acts as discriminatory), a multiracial feminist approach offers additional interpretations: Interpersonal interactions are shaped by intersecting hierarchies of gender and race; controlling images of racial minority groups often invoke gender, sexual, class and age-based stereotypes; gender bias is built into our measures and models of discrimination.

It is true that survey research produced with an essentialistic perspective on gender, race, and sexuality may be difficult to reconcile, fully with multiracial feminism. Some surveys, including the National Black Feminist Study (NBFS), do not ask respondents to identify their gender, relying instead on the interviewer's assessment. Others ask about sex but not gender or vice versa—the implication being that the two are synonymous. But, as I have tried to document here, research produced from these surveys can nonetheless help us to understand the social world, particularly when researchers approach the project with a multiracial feminist perspective. There may not be one clear way to "queer a survey" (Williams, 2006, p. 456), but bringing a multiracial feminist perspective to survey research is certainly a step in the right direction.

Re-thinking Our Aims: What Is Post-Positivist Survey Research?

In her recent work on feminist methodology, sociologist Joey Sprague begins with a critique of *positivism*, which, she argues, underpins much of contemporary social science research. As a theory of knowledge, positivism is the belief that "the world of experience is an objective world, governed by underlying regularities, [and] even natural laws" (Sprague, 2005, p. 32). Social researchers who embrace positivism hold that "if we systematically and dispassionately observe the data of the empirical world, we can detect the lawful patterns of which they are evidence." For Sprague and many other feminist scholars, one of the central limitations of positivism is its failure to understand scientific pursuits as both conceived and practiced within a broader social and historical context.[iv] As Sprague writes, "the central criticism of positivism is directed at the notion that scientists can occupy an Archimedean point outside the ongoing swim of the social world, escaping its influence as they develop hypotheses, make their measurements, analyze the data, and draw conclusions."[v] Identifying the "cultural elements" that are built into scientific practices at any historical moment and considering how cultural elements may shape our findings are critical to post-positivist feminist research (Harding, 1998).

Many feminist scholars operating from a post-positivist perspective see value in scientific pursuits, but they simultaneously emphasize that these pursuits must be understood as culturally grounded (e.g., Harding, 1998; Risman, 2001; Sprague, 2005). This is not to say that all knowledge

---

[iv] For example, see Harding (1987), Risman (1993), Sprague and Kobrynowicz (2004).

[v] Here Sprague is drawing from Smith (1987), but see also Harding (2004, p. 55).

claims are equally legitimate (i.e., an acceptance of relativism) but, rather, that from the moment we researchers conceive of our research questions through the time when readers reflect on our findings and conclusions, we are all drawing from cultural understandings of the world around us. Acknowledging the cultural foundations of scientific research opens the door for multiple scientific narratives to emerge. Rather than aspiring to rid our scientific pursuits from culture and subjectivity, clinging to the "possibility of value-free singular context-less Truth," post-positivist feminist researchers highlight the ways in which our culture, and our social locations within the cultural landscape, influence our research (Risman, 2001, p. 601). And doing so often reveals underlying systems of inequality.[vi] Moreover, identifying the cultural processes at work in scientific research can potentially *increase* the quality of scientific research. As feminist philosopher Sandra Harding (1991, p. 149) explains, "If the goal is to make available for critical scrutiny all the evidence marshaled for or against a scientific hypothesis, then this evidence too requires critical examination within scientific research processes. In other words, we can think of strong objectivity as extending the notion of scientific research to include systematic examination of such powerful background beliefs."

Though not often explicitly linked, feminist critiques of positivism go hand in hand with multiracial feminist methodology. Scholars from both approaches highlight the inequalities embedded within the knowledge production process, and both advocate scholarly research that is more self-reflective and inclusive. As Warner (2008, p. 462) explains, intersectionality can help psychologists "to pay attention to and be critical not only of the questions they ask and the phenomena they test, but also the questions they do not ask and the phenomena they do not test." "Truly," she writes, "one of the central issues in the study of intersectionality is that of visibility—who is granted attention, who is not, and the consequences of these actions for the study of social issues." Both multiracial feminist and post-positivist approaches see value in listening to diverse perspectives and searching for multiple narratives. Both also encourage scholars to expand our circles of accountability—to hold ourselves accountable to something beyond disciplinary norms and expectations.

Expanding the Field of Critical Research: How Do We Move Across Disciplinary Boundaries?

Grounding survey research in multiracial feminist scholarship provides a different vantage point from which to identify the "cultural elements"

[vi] See, for example, Hartsock (1983/2003); Kessler (1998); Smith (1987); Sprague (2005).

that shape scientific inquiry (Harding, 1998), but doing so requires moving beyond narrow disciplinary boundaries. As shown in Chapter 2, researchers approach survey research in a variety of different ways, and our methods and theoretical frameworks are largely related to the disciplinary context in which we produce our work. And while disciplinary approaches are no doubt useful for a variety of research projects, narrowly conceived disciplinary approaches simultaneously work to "enforce conventions, sustain hierarchies and mechanisms of exclusion, and police boundaries" (Thorne, 2006, p. 477). In other words, when we produce research from within a disciplined approach, it is far too easy to continue to do things as they are typically done. And if there are oversights, misrepresentations, and inequalities built into the most commonly used techniques, then relying on disciplinary norms can perpetuate these inequalities.

A multiracial feminist approach challenges these inequalities by encouraging scholars to broaden our scholarly spheres of accountability—to expand the intellectual and political communities to which we hold ourselves accountable. This means crossing over disciplinary borders to engage in dialogue with scholars in other disciplines, as well as communities underrepresented in academics. As Sprague (2005, p. 198) writes, "we need to construct our discourse as critical conversations among people operating from different standpoints. . . . We must be willing to use our disagreements with other scholars as points of access to improved understanding." And because interdisciplinarity *expands*, rather than *replaces*, traditional circles of accountability, survey research grounded in multiracial feminist theorizing is well positioned to strengthen scientific research. As Harding (2004, p. 43) explains, "knowledge claims are always socially situated, and the failure by dominant groups critically and systematically to interrogate their advantaged social situation and the effect of such advantages on their beliefs leaves the social situation a scientifically and epistemologically disadvantaged one for generating knowledge." Rather than undermining scientific pursuits, expanding the field of critical research and diversifying the perspectives represented can enhance future social science research.

But as we have seen, achieving interdisciplinarity is a difficult task. And despite feminist scholars' rhetorical commitment to interdisciplinary scholarship, much feminist scholarship remains mired in distinctly disciplined approaches. While some have suggested that the lack of interdisciplinarity in feminist scholarship is attributable to vast methodological differences (i.e., quantitative and qualitative approaches), my analysis of feminist survey research casts doubt on this explanation.[vii] Contemporary feminist

---

[vii] See, for example, McCall (2005).

survey research is largely produced within academic institutions, where accountability is structured almost exclusively by academic disciplines (for example, by disciplinary tenure lines, disciplinary evaluation committees, and hierarchical rankings of disciplinary journals). And without institutional support for interdisciplinary spaces, it is likely that feminist dialogues will remain structured by disciplinary differences (Allen & Kitch, 1998). Feminist survey researchers in political science, sociology, and psychology are already fully capable of reading each other's work, yet citation patterns within these fields remain largely structured by disciplinary boundaries. In other words, citation patterns reflect disciplinary accountability. And this narrow circle of accountability impedes the development of a multiracial feminist approach to survey research.

Conclusion

Discussing the methodological implications of feminist theories, sociologist Barbara Risman (1993, p. 24) writes,

> One can take a feminist perspective and epistemological concerns and incorporate them into any methodological technique. And one can ignore feminist insights and agendas in any methodological tradition. As long as so many feminists continue to presume quantitative methodology is necessarily naively positivist, feminist scholarship will remain at the periphery of many substantive areas where mainstream scholarship has become highly quantified.

The same holds true for multiracial feminism and social science survey research. The presumption that multiracial feminism and quantitative analyses of survey research are incompatible and, therefore, can offer each other nothing does little to advance feminist scholarship or social science research. Instead, it solidifies the borders separating the humanities and the social sciences, the quantitative and qualitative, the empirical and theoretical. But if, as Vivian May (2002, p. 134–135) suggests, we understand contemporary women's studies as "an area of inquiry and knowledge production that resists closure, invites conversation, and promotes a reflexive capacity for 'ongoing reinterpretation' and accountability," then the project of multiracial feminist survey research becomes much more feasible.[viii]

Individually, each of the chapters here presents a different approach to bringing a multiracial feminist perspective to survey research. It is my hope,

---

[viii] In speaking of "ongoing reinterpretation," May is drawing from Lorraine Code (1995, p. 135)

however, that, collectively, these chapters offer something more than a series of specific analytic interventions. I have argued that multiracial feminism offers a new approach for viewing and doing survey research and that an interdisciplinary multiracial feminist perspective can ultimately increase the quality of social science survey research. What would it look like if we deliberately grounded our survey research in interdisciplinary multiracial feminist theorizing? Here I have outlined some possibilities, but there are undoubtedly others, and I look forward to seeing their development in future research.

References and Further Readings

Allen, J. A., & Kitch, S. L. (1998). Disciplined by disciplines? The need for an interdisciplinary research mission in women's studies. *Feminist Studies, 24,* 275–299.

Allison, P. (1999). *Multiple regression: A primer.* Thousand Oaks, CA: Pine Forge.

Allport, G. W. (1954). *The nature of prejudice.* Cambridge, MA: Addison-Wesley.

Aronson, P. (2003). Feminists or "postfeminists"? Young women's attitudes toward feminism and gender relations. *Gender & Society, 17,* 903–922.

Ayres M. M., Friedman C. K., & Leaper, C. (2009). Individual and situational factors related to young women's likelihood of confronting sexism in their everyday lives. *Sex Roles, 61,* 449–460.

Baca Zinn, M., Hondagneu-Sotelo, P., & Messner, M. (2007). Gender through the prism of difference. In M. L. Andersen & P. Hill Collins (Eds.), *Race, class & gender: An anthology* (pp. 147–156). Belmont, CA: Wadsworth. (Original work published 2000)

Baca Zinn, M., & Thornton Dill, B. (1996). Theorizing difference from multiracial feminism. *Feminist Studies, 22,* 321–333.

Barad, K. (2007). *Meeting the universe halfway.* Durham, NC: Duke University Press.

Barkley Brown, E. (1992). What has happened here? The politics of difference in women's history and feminist politics. *Feminist Studies, 18,* 295–312.

Bay-Cheng, L. Y., & Zucker, A. N. (2007). Feminism between the sheets: Sexual attitudes among feminists, nonfeminists, and egalitarians. *Psychology of Women Quarterly, 31,* 157–163.

Beale, F. (1970). Double jeopardy: To be black and female. In R. Morgan (Ed.), *Sisterhood is powerful* (pp. 340–352). New York: Random House.

Beauboeuf-Lafontant, T. (2009). *Behind the mask of the strong black woman.* Philadelphia: Temple University Press.

Berger, M. T. (2004). *Workable sisterhood: The political journey of stigmatized women with HIV/AIDS.* Princeton, NJ: Princeton University Press.

Berger, M. T., & Guidroz, K. (2009). *The intersectional approach: Transforming the academy through race, class, and gender.* Chapel Hill, NC: University of North Carolina Press.

Berger, M. T., & Radeloff, C. (2011). *Transforming scholarship: Why women's and gender studies students are changing themselves and the world.* New York: Routledge.

Blee, K., & Tickamyer, A. (1995). Racial differences in men's attitudes about women's gender roles. *Journal of Marriage and the Family, 57,* 21–30.

Bolzendahl, C. I., & Myers, D. J. (2004). Feminist attitudes and support for gender equality: Opinion change in women and men, 1974–1998. *Social Forces, 83,* 759–790.

Booth, K. (2004). *Local women, global science.* Bloomington: Indiana University Press.

Breines, W. (2006). *The trouble between us: An uneasy history of white and black women in the feminist movement.* Oxford, UK: Oxford University Pres.

Broman, C. L., Mavaddat, R., & Hsu, S. (2000). The experience and consequences of perceived racial discrimination: A study of African Americans. *Journal of Black Psychology, 26,* 165–180.

Buchanan, N. T., & Ormerod, A. (2002). Racialized sexual harassment in the lives of African American women. *Women & Therapy, 25,* 107–124.

Buchanan, N. T., Settles, I. H., & Woods, K. C. (2008). Comparing sexual harassment subtypes among black and white women by military rank: Double jeopardy, the jezebel, and the cult of true womanhood. *Psychology of Women Quarterly, 32,* 347–361.

Bullock, H. E., & Fernald, J. L. (2003). "Feminism lite?" Feminist identification, speaker appearance, and perceptions of feminist and antifeminist messengers. *Psychology of Women Quarterly, 27,* 291–299.

Buschman, J. K., & Lenart, S. (1996). "I am not a feminist, but . . .": College women, feminism, and negative experiences. *Political Psychology, 17,* 59–75.

Butler, J. 1990. *Gender trouble.* New York: Routledge.

Caldwell, C. H., Guthrie, B. J., & Jackson, J. S. (2006). Identity development, discrimination, and psychological well-being among African American and Caribbean black adolescents. In A. J. Schulz & L. Mullings (Eds.), *Gender, race, class, and health: Intersectional approaches* (pp. 163–191). San Francisco: Jossey-Bass.

Caldwell, K. (2007). *Negras in Brazil: Re-envisioning black women, citizenship, and the politics of identity.* Piscataway, NJ: Rutgers University Press.

Carbert, L. I. (1994). Conceptualization of feminism among Ontario farm women *Journal of Women and Politics, 14,* 19–42.

Chafetz, J. S. (2004a). Bridging feminist theory and research methodology. *Journal of Family Issues, 25,* 963–977.

Chafetz, J. S. (2004b). Some thoughts by an unrepentant "positivist" who considers herself a feminist nonetheless. In S. N. Hesse-Biber & M. L. Yaiser (Eds.), *Feminist perspectives on social research* (pp. 320–329). New York: Oxford University Press.

Chamberlain, L. J., Crowley, M., Tope, D., & Hodson, R. (2008). Sexual harassment in organizational context. *Work and Occupations, 35,* 262–295.

Christian, B. (1995). The race for theory. In G. Anzaldúa (Ed.), *Making face, making soul=Haciendo caras: Creative and critical perspectives by feminists of color* (pp. 335–345). San Francisco: Aunt Lute Books. (Original work published 1990)

Code, L. (1995). *Rhetorical spaces: Essays on gendered locations.* New York: Routledge.

Cohen, C. (1997). Punks, bulldaggers, and welfare queens: The radical potential of queer politics? *GLQ: A Journal of Lesbian and Gay Studies, 3,* 437–465.

Cole, E. R., & Zucker, A. N. (2007). Black and white women's perspectives on femininity. *Cultural Diversity and Ethnic Minority Psychology, 13,* 1–9.

Combahee River Collective. (1981). A black feminist statement. In C. Moraga & G. Anzaldua, (Eds.), *This bridge called my back* (pp. 210–218).Watertown, MA: Persephone Press.

Connell, R. W. (1992). A very straight gay: Masculinity, homosexual experience, and the dynamics of gender. *American Sociological Review, 57,* 735–751.

Cook, E. A. (1989). Measuring feminist consciousness. *Women & Politics, 9,* 71–88.

Cook, J. A. (1983). An interdisciplinary look at feminist methodology: Ideas and practice in sociology, history, and anthropology. *Humboldt Journal of Social Relations, 10,* 127–152.

Cortina, L. M. (2001). Assessing sexual harassment among Latinas: Development of an instrument. *Cultural Diversity and Ethnic Minority Psychology, 7,* 164–181.

Crenshaw, K. (1991). Mapping the margins: Intersectionality, identity politics, and violence against women of color. *Stanford Law Review, 43,* 1241–1299.

Crenshaw, K. (1992). Race, gender, and sexual harassment. *Southern California Law Review, 65,* 1467–1476.

Davis, A. (1983). *Women, Race, and Class.* New York: Random House. (Original work published 1981)

Davis, K. (2008). Intersectionality as buzzword: A sociology of science perspective on what makes a feminist theory successful. *Feminist Theory, 9,* 67–85.

Denis, A. (2008). Intersectional analysis: A contribution of feminism to sociology. *International Sociology, 35,* 677–694.

DeSantis, A. D. (2007). *Inside Greek U.* Lexington: University Press of Kentucky.

Dugger, K. (1988). Social location and gender-role attitudes: A comparison of black and white women. *Gender & Society, 2,* 425–448.

Espiritu, Y. L. (1997). *Asian American women and men.* Walnut Creek, CA: AltaMira Press.

Essed, P. (1991). *Understanding everyday racism: An interdisciplinary theory.* Newbury Park, CA: Sage.

Essed, P. (2001). *Towards a methodology to identify converging forms of everyday discrimination.* Paper presented at the UN Commission on the Status of Women. Retrieved January 22, 2011, from http://www.un.org/womenwatch/daw/csw/essed45.htm

Faludi, S. (1992). *Backlash: The undeclared war against American women.* New York: Anchor Books.

Fausto-Sterling, A. (2000). The five sexes, revisited. *Sciences, 40,* 18–23.

Feagin, J. R. (1991). The continuing significance of race: Antiblack discrimination in public places. *American Sociological Review, 56,* 101–116.

Feagin, J. R., & Eckberg, D. L. (1980). Discrimination: Motivation, action, effects, and context. *Annual Review of Sociology, 6,* 1–20.

Fine, M. (1985). Reflections on a feminist psychology: Paradoxes and prospects. *Psychology of Women Quarterly, 9*, 167–183.

Fine, M. (1992). *Disruptive voices: The possibilities of feminist research.* Ann Arbor: University of Michigan Press.

Finger, A., & Rosner, V. 2001. Introduction (to this vol. of journal). *Feminist Studies, 27*, 499–503.

Fingeret, M. C., & Gleaves, D. H. (2004). Sociocultural, feminist, and psychological influences on women's body satisfaction: A structural modeling analysis. *Psychology of Women Quarterly, 28*, 370–380.

Fitzgerald, L. F. (1993). Sexual harassment: Violence against women in the workplace. *American Psychologist, 48*, 1070–1076.

Fonow, M. M., & Cook, J. A. (1991). *Beyond methodology: Feminist scholarship as lived research.* Bloomington: Indiana University Press.

Fonow, M. M., & Cook, J. A. (2005). Feminist methodology: New applications in the academy and public policy. *Signs, 30*, 2211–2236.

Forman, T., Williams, D. R., & Jackson, J. S. (1997). Race, place, and discrimination. *Perspectives on Social Problems, 9*, 231–261.

Friedman, S. S. (1998). (Inter)disciplinarity and the question of the women's studies Ph.D. *Feminist Studies, 24*, 301–325.

Frye, M. (1983). *Politics of reality: Essays in feminist theory.* Trumansburg, NY: Crossing Press.

Glenn, E. N. (2002). *Unequal freedom: How race and gender shaped American citizenship and labor.* Cambridge, MA: Harvard University Press.

Glick, P., & Fiske, S. T. (1996). The ambivalent sexism inventory: Differentiating hostile and benevolent sexism, *Journal of Personality and Social Psychology, 70*, 491–512.

Gordon, L. (1991). Comments on *That noble dream. American Historical Review, 96*, 683–687.

Graham, H. (1983). Do her answers fit his questions? Women and the survey method. In E. Gamarnikow, D. Morgan, J. Purvis, & D. Taylorson (Eds.), *The public and the private* (pp. 132–147). London: Heinemann.

Gruber, J. E., & Bjorn, L. (1988). Routes to a feminist orientation among women auto workers. *Gender & Society, 2*, 496–509.

Hancock, A. (2007). When multiplication doesn't equal quick addition: Examining intersectionality as a research paradigm. *Perspectives on Politics, 5*, 63–79.

Haraway, D. (1988). Situated knowledges: The science question in feminism and the privilege of partial perspective. *Feminist Studies, 14*, 575–599.

Haraway, D. (1990). A manifesto for cyborgs: Science, technology, and socialist feminism in the last quarter. In L. Nicholson (Ed.). *Feminism and postmodernism* (pp. 580–671). New York: Routledge.

Harding, S. (1987). *Feminism and methodology.* Bloomington: Indiana University Press.

Harding, S. (1991). *Whose science? Whose knowledge? Thinking from women's lives.* Ithaca, New York: Cornell University Press.

Harding, S. (1998). *Is science multicultural?: Postcolonialisms, feminisms, and epistemologies.* Bloomington: Indiana University Press.

Harding, S. (2004). Rethinking standpoint epistemology: What is strong objectivity? In S. Hesse-Biber & M. L. Yaiser (Eds.), *Feminist perspectives on social research*, (pp. 39–64). New York: Oxford University Press. (Original work published 1993)

Harnois, C. E. (2005). Different paths to different feminisms? Bridging multiracial feminist theory with quantitative sociological gender research. *Gender & Society, 19*, 809–828.

Harnois, C. E. (2008). Representing feminism: Past, present & future. *National Women's Studies Association Journal, 20*, 120–145.

Harnois, C. E., & Ifatunji, M. (2011). Gendered measures, gendered models: Toward an intersectional analysis of interpersonal racial discrimination. *Ethnic and Racial Studies, 34*, 1006–1028.

Hartsock, N. (2003). The feminist standpoint. In S. Harding & M. H. Dordrecth (Eds.), *Discovering reality* (pp. 283–310). The Netherlands: Kluwer Academic. (Original work published 1983)

Hawkesworth, M. (2006). *Feminist inquiry*. New Brunswick, NJ: Rutgers University Press.

Henley, N. M., Meng, K., O'Brien, D., McCarthy, W. J., & Sockloskie, R. J. (1998). Developing a scale to measure the diversity of feminist attitudes. *Psychology of Women Quarterly, 22*, 317–348.

Henley, N. M., Spalding, L. R., & Kosta, A. (2000). Development of the short form of the Feminist Perspectives Scale. *Psychology of Women Quarterly, 24*, 254–256.

Hesse-Biber, S. N. (Ed.). (2007). *Handbook of feminist research: Theory and praxis*. Thousand Oaks, CA: Sage.

Hesse-Biber, S. N., Gilmartin, C., & Lydenberg, R. (Eds.). (1999). *Feminist approaches to theory and methodology: An interdisciplinary reader*. New York: Oxford University Press.

Hesse-Biber, S. N., & Yaiser, M. L. (Eds.). (2004). *Feminist perspectives on social research*. New York: Oxford University Press.

Hewamanne, S. (2008). *Stitching identities in a free trade zone: gender and politics in Sri Lanka*. Philadelphia: University of Pennsylvania Press.

Hewitt, N. (1992). Compounding differences. *Feminist Studies, 18*, 313–326.

Hill, C., & Silva, E. (2005). *Drawing the line: Sexual harassment on campus*. American Association of University Women. Retrieved December 28, 2010, from http://www.aauw.org/learn/research/all.cfm

Hill Collins, P. (1991). The meaning of motherhood in black culture and mother-daughter relationships. In P. Bell-Scott, B. Guy-Sheftall, J. J. Royster, J. Sims-Wood, M. De-Costa-Willis, & L. Fultz (Eds.), *Double stitch: Black women write about mothers and daughters* (pp. 42–60). Boston: Beacon Press.

Hill Collins, P. (2000). *Black feminist thought*. New York: Routledge. (Original work published 1990)

Hill Collins, P. (2004). *Black sexual politics*. New York: Routledge.

Hill Collins, P. (2006). What's in a name? Womanism, black feminism, and beyond. In L. Phillips (Ed.), *The womanist reader* (pp. 57–68). New York: Routledge. (Original work published 1996)

hooks, b. (1984). *Feminist theory: From margin to center*. Boston: South End Press.

hooks, b. (2004). *We real cool: Black men and masculinity*. New York: Routledge.

Huddy, L., Neely, F. K., & LaFay, M. R. (2000). The polls—Trends: Support for the women's movement. *Public Opinion Quarterly, 64*, 309–350.

Hudson-Weems, C. (2001). Africana womanism: The flip side of a coin. *Western Journal of Black Studies, 25*, 137–145.

Hudson-Weems, C. (2006). Africana womanism. In L. Phillips (Ed.), *The womanist reader* (pp. 44–54). New York: Routledge. (Original work published 1993)

Hunter, A., & Sellers, S. L. (1998). Feminist attitudes among African American women and men. *Gender & Society, 12*, 81–99.

Jaccard, J. 2001. *Interaction effects in logistic regression*. Thousand Oaks: Sage Publications.

Jackman, M. (1994). *The velvet glove: Paternalism and conflict in gender, class, and race relations*. Berkeley: University of California Press.

Jackson, J. S., Caldwell, C., Williams, D. R., Neighbors, H. W., Nesse, R. W., Taylor, R. J., & Trierweiler, S. J. (n.d.). *National survey of American life (NSAL), 2001–2003*. Ann Arbor: University of Michigan, Survey Research Center (ICPSR Study No. 00190). Retrieved from http://www.icpsr.umich.edu/icpsrweb/ICPSR/studies/00190/detail

Jackson, J. S., Caldwell, C., Williams, D. R., Neighbors, H. W., Nesse, R. W., Taylor, R. J., & Trierweiler, S. J. (n.d.). *National survey of American life self-administered questionnaire (NSAL-SAQ), February 2001–June 2003* [Computer file No. ICPSR27121-v1]. Ann Arbor, MI: Inter-university Consortium for Political and Social Research. doi:10.3886/ICPSR27121.v1

Jaggar, A. M. (2008). *Just methods: An interdisciplinary feminist reader*. Boulder, CO: Paradigm.

Jang, Y., Chiriboga, D. A., & Small, B. J. (2008). Perceived discrimination and psychological well-being: The mediating and moderating role of sense of control. *International Journal of Aging and Human Development, 66*, 213–227.

Jones, B. W. (1984). Race, sex, and class: Black female tobacco workers in Durham, North Carolina, 1920-1940, and the development of the female consciousness. *Feminist Studies, 10*, 441–451.

Jordan, J. (2003). Report from the Bahamas, 1982. *Meridians: feminism, race, transnationalism, 3*(2), 6–16. (Original work published 1982)

Kane, E. (2000). Racial and ethnic variations in gender-related attitudes. *Annual Review of Sociology, 26*, 419–439.

Kanter, R. M. (1993). *Men and women of the corporation*. New York: Basic Books. (Original work published 1977)

Kelley, R. D. G. (1995). Confessions of a nice Negro, or why I shaved my head. In D. Belton (Ed.), *Speak my name: Black men on masculinity and the American dream* (pp. 12–22). Boston: Beacon Press.

Kessler, R. C., Mickelson, K. D., & Williams, D. R. (1999). The prevalence, distribution, and mental health correlates of perceived discrimination in the United States. *Journal of Health and Social Behavior, 40*, 208–230.

Kessler, S. (1998). *Lessons from the intersexed.* New Brunswick, NJ: Rutgers University Press.

Kimmel, E. B., & Garko, M. G. (1995). Ethnic diversity in the experience of feminism: An existential–phenomenological approach. In H. Landrine (Ed.), *Bringing cultural diversity to feminist psychology: Theory, research, and practice* (pp. 27–53). Washington, DC: American Psychological Association.

King, D. K. (1988). Multiple jeopardy, multiple consciousness: The context of a black feminist ideology. *Signs, 14,* 42–72.

Klonoff, E. A., & Landrine, H. (1995). The schedule of sexist events. *Psychology of Women Quarterly, 19,* 439–470.

Klonoff E. A., Landrine H., & Campbell R. (2000). Sexist discrimination may account for well-known gender differences in psychiatric symptoms. *Psychology of Women Quarterly, 24,* 93–99.

Kohlman, M. H. (2006). Intersection theory: A more elucidating paradigm of quantitative analysis. *Race, Gender & Class, 13,* 42–59.

Kyungwon Hong, G. (2008). The future of our worlds: Black feminism and the politics of knowledge in the university under globalization. *Meridians: feminism, race, transnationalism, 127,* 95–115.

Landrine, H., Klonoff, E. A., & Brown-Collins, A. (1995). Cultural diversity and methodology in feminist psychology: Critique, proposal, empirical example. In H. Landrine (Ed.), *Bringing cultural diversity to feminist psychology: Theory, research, and practice* (pp. 55–75). Washington, DC: American Psychological Association.

Landrine, H., Klonoff, E. A., Gibbs, J., Manning, V., & Lund, M. (1995). Physical and psychiatric correlate of gender discrimination: An application of the schedule of sexist events. *Psychology of Women Quarterly, 19,* 473–492.

Lerner, G. (1979). *The majority finds its past.* Oxford, UK: Oxford University Press.

Lewis-Beck, M. S., Bryman, A. & Liao, T. F. (2004). *Sage encyclopedia of social science research methods.* Thousand Oaks, CA: Sage.

L'Heureux-Dubé, (Madam Justice) C. (1993). Writing for the minority in Canada (A.G.) v. Mossop, 1 S.C.R. 554 at 645–646.

Liss, M., Hoffner, C., & Crawford, M. (2000). What do feminists believe? *Psychology of Women Quarterly, 24,* 279–284.

Liss, M., O'Connor, C., Morosky, E., & Crawford, M. (2001). What makes a feminist? Predictors and correlates of feminist social identity in college women. *Psychology of Women Quarterly, 25,* 124–133.

Lorber, J. (1994). *Paradoxes of gender.* New Haven, CT: Yale University Press.

Lorde, A. (1984). *Sister outsider.* Trumansburg, NY: Crossing Press.

Ludvig, A. (2006, August). Differences between women? Intersecting voices in a female narrative. *European Journal of Women's Studies, 13,* 245–258.

Mann, S. A., & Huffman, D. J. (2004). The decentering of second wave feminism and the rise of the third wave. *Science and Society, 69,* 56–91.

Mannheim, K. (1952). The Problem of Generations. In Paul Kecskemeti (Ed.), *Essays on the Sociology of Knowledge* (276-332). London: Routledge and Kegan Paul. Original work published 1926.

Martin, P. Y., & Hummer, R. A. (1989). Fraternities and rape on campus. *Gender & Society, 3*, 457–473.

Martin, P. Y., Reynolds, J. R., & Keith, S. (2002). Gender bias and feminist consciousness among judges and attorneys: A standpoint theory analysis. *Signs: Journal of Women in Culture and Society, 27*, 665–701.

Matteson, A. V., & Moradi, B. (2005). Examining the structure of the schedule of sexist events: A replication and extension. *Psychology of Women Quarterly, 29*, 47–57.

May, V. (2002). Disciplinary desires and undisciplined daughters: Negotiating the politics of a women's studies doctoral education. *National Women's Studies Association Journal, 14*, 134–159.

May, V. (2010, November 12). *Intersectionality & outsider feminisms, or, "how many times has this all been said before?"* Presentation at the annual meeting of the National Women's Studies Association, Atlanta, Georgia.

McCabe, J. (2005). What's in a label? The relationship between feminist self-identification and "feminist" attitudes among U.S. women and men. *Gender & Society, 19*, 480–505.

McCall, L. (2005). The complexity of intersectionality. *Signs: Journal of Women in Culture and Society, 30*, 1771–1800.

McDermott, P. (1994). The risks and responsibilities of feminist academic journals. *National Women's Studies Association Journal, 6*, 373–383.

Moraga, C. (1983). La Güera. In C. Moraga & G. Anzaldúa (Eds.), *This bridge called my back: Writings by radical women of color* (pp. 27–34). New York: Kitchen Table Press. (Original work published 1981)

Moraga, C., & Anzaldúa, G. (Eds.). (1983). *This bridge called my back: Writings by radical women of color*. New York: Kitchen Table Press. (Original work published 1981)

Moya, P. M. L. (2001). Chicana feminism and postmodernist theory. *Signs: Journal of Women in Culture and Society, 26*, 441–483.

Naples, N. (2003). *Feminism and method: Ethnography, discourse analysis, and activist research*. New York: Routledge.

Naples, N., & Desai, M. (Eds.). (2002). *Women's activism and globalization: Linking local struggles and transnational politics*. New York: Routledge.

National Black Feminist Study. (2004–2005). Center for Survey Research & Analysis/UCONN Poll (No. 2004-FEM, Study No. USCSRA2004-FEM [Sponsored by Evelyn M. Simien. Acquired from the Roper Center for Public Opinion Research]). Mansfield, CT: University of Connecticut.

National Research Council. (2004). *Measuring racial discrimination* [Panel on methods for assessing discrimination (Committee on National Statistics, Division of Behavioral and Social Sciences and Education)]. R. M. Blank, M. Dabady, & C. F. Citro (Eds.). Washington, DC: National Academies Press.

Ntiri, D. W. (2001). Reassessing Africana womanism: Continuity and change. *Western Journal of Black Studies, 25*, 163–167.

Nutt, R. L. (2004). Prejudice and discrimination against women based on gender bias. In J. L. Chin (Ed.), *The psychology of prejudice and discrimination* (pp. 1–26). Westport, CT: Greenwood.

Okin, S. M. (1999). Is multiculturalism bad for women? In J. Cohen, M. Howard, & M. C. Nussbaum(Eds.), *Is multiculturalism bad for women?* (pp. 9–24). Princeton, NJ: Princeton University Press.

Omi, M., & Winant, H. (1994). *Racial formation in the United States from the 1960s to the 1990s.* New York: Routledge.

Ontario Human Rights Commission. (2001). *An intersectional approach to discrimination: Addressing multiple grounds in human rights claims.* Retrieved December 28, 2010, from http://www.ohrc.on.ca

Pager, D., & Sheperd, H. (2008). The sociology of discrimination: Racial discrimination in employment, housing, credit, and consumer markets. *Annual Review of Sociology, 34*, 181–209.

Peltola, P., Milkie, M. A., & Presser, S. (2004). The "feminist" mystique: Feminist identity in three generations of women. *Gender & Society, 18*, 122–144.

Pesquera, B. M., & Segura, D. A. (1993). There is no going back: Chicanas and feminism. In N. Alarcon, R. Castro, E. Perez, B. Pesquera, A. S. Riddell, & P. Zavella (Eds.), *Chicana critical issues* (pp. 95–115). Berkeley, CA: Third Woman Press.

Phillips, L. (Ed.). (2006). *The womanist reader.* New York: Routledge.

Pierce, J. (2010). *"Your Maria's a real hot tamale": Racialization, sexualization, and desexualization of women legal workers.* Paper presented at the Annual Meeting of the American Sociological Association, Atlanta, Georgia.

Porter Gump, J. (1980). Reality and myth: Employment and sex-role ideology in black women. In J. Sherman & F. L. Denmark (Eds.), *The psychology of women: Directions in research* (pp. 349–380). New York: Psychological Dimensions.

Pryse, M. (2000). Trans/feminist methodology: Bridges to interdisciplinary thinking. *National Women's Studies Association Journal, 12*, 105–118.

Purdie-Vaughns, V., & Eibach, R. P. (2008). Intersectional invisibility: The ideological sources and social consequences of the non-prototypicality of intersectional subordinates. *Sex Roles, 59*, 377–391.

Purvis, J. (2004). Grrrls and women together in the third wave: Embracing the challenges of intergenerational feminism(s). *National Women's Studies Association Journal, 16*, 93–123.

Quillian, L. (2006). New approaches to understanding racial prejudice and discrimination. *Annual Review of Sociology, 32*, 299–328.

Ransford, E., & Miller, J. (1983). Race, sex, and feminist outlooks. *American Sociological Review, 48*, 46–59.

Reinharz, S. (1992). *Feminist methods in social research.* New York: Oxford University Press.

Rhodebeck, L. A. (1996). The structure of men's and women's feminist orientations: Feminist identity and feminist opinion. *Gender & Society, 10*, 386–403.

Ricketts, M. (1989). Epistemological values of feminists in psychology. *Psychology of Women Quarterly, 13*, 401–415.

Ridgeway, C. L., & England, P. (2007). Sociological approaches to sex discrimination in employment. In F. J. Crosby, M. S. Stockdale, & A. S. Ropp, (Eds.), *Sex discrimination in the workplace: Multidisciplinary perspectives* (pp. 189–211). Oxford, UK: Blackwell.

Ridley Malson, M. (1983). Black women's sex roles: The social context for a new ideology. *Journal of Social Issues, 39*, 101–113.

Risman, B. J. (1993). Methodological implications of feminist scholarship. *American Sociologist, 24*, 15–25.

Risman, B. J. (2001). A comment on the biological limits of gender construction: Calling the bluff on value-free science. *American Sociological Review, 66*, 605–611.

Risman, B. J., Sprague, J., & Howard, J. (1993). Comment on Francesca M. Cancian's "Feminist science." *Gender & Society, 7*, 608–609.

Roscigno, V. (2007). *The face of discrimination*. New York: Rowman & Littlefield.

Roth, B. (2004). *Separate roads to feminism: Black, Chicana, and white feminist movements in America's second wave*. Cambridge, UK: Cambridge University Press.

Rowe, A. C. (2005). Be longing: Toward a feminist politics of relation. *National Women's Studies Association Journal, 17*, 15–46.

Rubin, L. R., Nemeroff, C. J., & Russo, N. F. (2004). Exploring feminist women's body consciousness. *Psychology of Women Quarterly, 28*, 27–37.

Runyan, A. S., & Wenning, M. V. (2004). Prospect for renewed feminist activism in the heartland: A study of Daytonian women's politics. *National Women's Studies Association Journal, 16*, 180–214.

Russo, N. F. (1998). Measuring feminist attitudes: Just what does it mean to be a feminist? *Psychology of Women Quarterly, 22*, 313–315.

Sabik, N. J., & Tylka, T.L. (2006). Do feminist identity styles moderate the relation between perceived sexist events and disordered eating? *Psychology of Women Quarterly, 30*, 77–84.

Schick, V. R., Zucker, A.N., & Bay-Cheng, L. Y. (2008). Safer, better sex through feminism: The role of feminist ideology in women's sexual well-being. *Psychology of Women Quarterly, 32*, 225–232.

Schnittker, J., Freese, J., & Powell, B. (2003). Who are feminists and what do they believe? *American Sociological Review, 68*, 607–622.

Segura, D. (1994). Working at motherhood: Chicana and Mexican immigrant mothers and employment. In E. Nakano Glenn, G. Chang, & L. Rennie Forcey. (Eds.), *Mothering: Ideology, experience, and agency* (pp. 211–233). New York: Routledge.

Sellers, R. M., Caldwell, C. H., Schmeelk-Cone, K. H., & Zimmerman, M. A. 2003. Racial identity, racial discrimination, perceived stress, and psychological distress among African American young adults. *Journal of Health and Social Behavior, 43*, 302–317.

Sellers, R. M., & Shelton, J. N. (2003). The role of racial identity in perceived racial discrimination. *Journal of Personality and Social Psychology, 84*, 1079–1092.

Sherif, C. W. (1987). Bias in psychology. In S. G. Harding (Ed.), *Feminism and methodology: Social science issues* (pp. 1–14). Bloomington: Indiana University Press. (Original work published 1979)

Shih, J. (2002). "Yeah, I could hire this one, but I know it's gonna be a problem": How race, nativity, and gender affect employers' perceptions of the manageability of job seekers. *Ethnic and Racial Studies, 25*, 99–119.

Siegel, D. L. (1997). Reading between the waves: Feminist historiography in a "postfeminist" moment. In L. Haywood & J. Dake (Eds.). *Third wave agenda* (pp. 55–82). Minneapolis: University of Minnesota Press.

Simien, E. M. (2004). Gender differences in attitudes toward black feminism among African Americans. *Political Science Quarterly, 119*, 315–338.

Simien, E. M. (2007). Doing intersectionality research: From conceptual issues to practical examples. *Politics & Gender, 3*, 36–43.

Singleton, R., & Straits, B. C. (1999). *Approaches to social research*. New York: Oxford University Press.

Smith, D. (1974). Women's Perspective as a radical critique of sociology. *Sociological Inquiry, 4*, 1–13.

Smith, B. (1980). Racism in women's studies. *Frontiers: A Journal of Women Studies, 5*, 48–49.

Smith, B. (Ed). (1983). *Homegirls: A black feminist anthology*. New York: Kitchen Table: Women of Color Press.

Smith, B., & Frazier, D. (1981). A black feminist statement. In C. Moraga & G. Anzaldua (Eds.), *This bridge called my back* (pp. 210–218).Watertown, MA: Persephone Press. (Original work published 1977)

Smith, D. E. (1987). *The everyday world as problematic: A feminist sociology*. Boston: Northeastern University Press.

Smith, T. W, Marsden, P., Hout, M., & Kim, J. (2011). *General social surveys, 1972–2010* [Machine-readable data file]. Chicago: University of Chicago, National Opinion Research Center.

Spelman, E. (1988). *Inessential woman*. Boston: Beacon Press.

Sprague, J. (2005). *Feminist methodologies for critical researchers: Bridging differences*. Walnut Creek, CA: AltaMira Press.

Sprague, J., & Kobrynowicz, D. (2004). A feminist epistemology. In S. N. Hesse-Biber & M. L. Yaiser (Eds.), *Feminist perspectives on social research* (pp. 78–98). New York: Oxford University Press.

Sprague, J., & Zimmerman, M. K. (1989). Quality and quantity: Reconstructing feminist methodology. *American Sociologist, 20*, 71–87.

Sprague, J., & Zimmerman, M. K. (1993). Overcoming dualisms: A feminist agenda for sociological methodology. In P. England (Ed.), *Theory on gender/feminism on theory* (pp. 255–280). Hawthorne, NY: Walter de Gruyter.

Springer, K. (2002). Third wave black feminism? *Signs, 27*, 1057–1082.

Stacey, J., & Thorne, B. (1985). The missing feminist revolution in sociology. *Social Problems, 32*, 301–316.

Stacey, J., & Thorne, B. (1996). Is sociology still missing its feminist revolution? *Perspectives: ASA Theory Section Newsletter, 18*, 1–3.

Stanley, L., & Wise, S. (1983). *Breaking out again: Feminist ontology and epistemology*. New York: Routledge & K. Paul.

Swami, V., & Tovée, M. J. (2006). The influence of body mass index on the physical attractiveness preferences of feminist and nonfeminist heterosexual women and lesbians. *Psychology of Women Quarterly, 30,* 252–257.

Taylor, V., Whittier, N., & Pelak, C. F. (2001). The women's movement: Persistence through transformation. In L. Richardson, V. Taylor, & N. Whitter (Eds.), *Feminist frontiers* (5th ed., pp. 559–574). New York: McGraw-Hill.

Texeira, M. T. (2002). "Who protects and serves me?" A case study of sexual harassment of African American women in one U.S. law enforcement agency. *Gender & Society, 16,* 524–545.

Thomas, A. J., Witherspoon, K. M., & Speight, S. L. (2008). Gendered racism, psychological distress, and coping styles of African American women. *Cultural Diversity & Ethnic Minority Psychology, 14,* 307–314.

Thompson, B. (2002). Multiracial feminism: Recasting the chronology of second wave feminism. *Feminist Studies, 28,* 336–360.

Thorne, B. (2006). How can feminist sociology sustain its critical edge? *Social Problems, 53,* 473–478.

Thornton Dill, B. (1988, March). Our mothers' grief: Racial ethnic women and the maintenance of families. *Journal of Family History, 13,* 415–431.

Thornton Dill, B., & Baca Zinn, M. (1997). Race and gender: Re-visioning the social sciences. In J. Ladenson, M. Anderson, L. Fine, & K. Geissler (Eds.). *Doing feminism: Teaching and research* (pp. 39–52). East Lansing: Michigan State University Press.

Thornton Dill, B., & Zambrana, R. (2009). *Emerging intersections: Race, class, and gender in theory, policy and practice.* Piscataway, NJ: Rutgers University Press.

Timberlake, J. M., & Estes, S. B. (2007). Do racial and ethnic stereotypes depend on the sex of the target group members? Evidence from a survey-based experiment. *Sociological Quarterly, 48,* 399–433.

Tong, R. P. (1998). *Feminist thought.* Boulder, CO: Westview.

Utsey, S. O., & Ponterotto, J. G. (1996). Development and validation of the index of race-related stress (IRRS). *Journal of Counseling Psychology, 43,* 490–502.

Valadez, J. (2001). Standpoint epistemology and women of color. In D. L. Hoeveler & J. K. Boles (Eds.), *Women of color: Defining the issues, hearing the voices* (pp. 69–80). Santa Barbara, CA: Greenwood Press.

Walker, A. (2006). Womanist. In L. Phillips (Ed.), *The womanist reader* (p. 19). New York: Routledge. (Original work published 1983)

Warner, L. R. (2008). A best practices guide to intersectional approaches in psychological research. *Sex Roles, 59,* 454–463.

Weber, L. (2001). *Understanding race, class, gender, and sexuality: A conceptual framework.* New York: McGraw-Hill.

Wiegman, R. (2002). *Women's studies on its own.* Durham, NC: Duke University Press.

Welsh, S., Carr, J., MacQuarrie, B., & Huntley, A. (2006). I'm not thinking of it as sexual harassment: Understanding harassment across race and citizenship. *Gender & Society, 20,* 87–107.

Westmarland, N. (2001, February). The quantitative/qualitative debate and feminist research: A subjective view of objectivity. *Forum: Qualitative Social Research*, 2(1), Article 13. Retrieved January 10, 2011, from http://www.qualitative-research.net/index.php/fqs/article/viewArticle/974/2124

Whittier, N. (1995). *Feminist generations*. Philadelphia: Temple University Press.

Williams, C. (2006). Still missing? Comments on the twentieth anniversary of "The missing feminist revolution in sociology." *Social Problems, 53*, 454–458.

Williams, D. R., Neighbors, H. W., & Jackson, J. S. (2003). Racial/ethnic discrimination and health: Findings from community studies. *American Journal of Public Health, 93*, 200–208.

Yoder, J. D., McDonald, T. W. (1998). Measuring sexist discrimination in the workplace: Support for the validity of the schedule of sexist events. *Psychology of Women Quarterly, 22*, 487–491.

Young, I. M. (2004). Gender as seriality: Thinking about women as a social collective. *Signs, 19*, 713–738.

Yuval-Davis, N. (2006). Intersectionality and feminist politics. *European Journal of Women's Studies, 13*, 193–209.

Zuberi, T. (2001). *Thicker than blood: How racial statistics lie*. Minneapolis: University of Minnesota Press.

Zuberi, T. (2008). Deracializing social statistics: Problems in the quantification of race. In T. Zuberi & E. Bonilla-Silva (Eds.), *White logic, white methods: Racism and methodology* (pp. 127–134). Lanham, MD: Rowman & Littlefield.

Zuberi, T. & Bonilla-Silva, E. (2008). Introduction. In T. Zuberi & E. Bonilla-Silva (Eds.), *White logic, white methods: Racism and methodology* (p. 6). Lanham, MD: Rowman & Littlefield.

Zuberi, T., & Bonilla-Silva, E. (Eds.). (2008). *White logic, white methods: Racism and methodology*. Lanham, MD: Rowman & Littlefield.

Author Index

Subject Index

Note: Page numbers in italics refer to tables and figures.

⑤SAGE research methods online

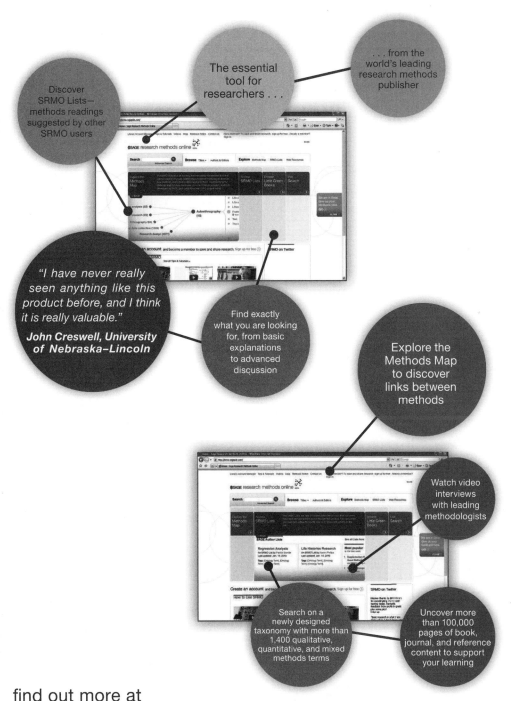

Discover SRMO Lists—methods readings suggested by other SRMO users

The essential tool for researchers . . .

. . . from the world's leading research methods publisher

"I have never really seen anything like this product before, and I think it is really valuable."

John Creswell, University of Nebraska–Lincoln

Find exactly what you are looking for, from basic explanations to advanced discussion

Explore the Methods Map to discover links between methods

Watch video interviews with leading methodologists

Search on a newly designed taxonomy with more than 1,400 qualitative, quantitative, and mixed methods terms

Uncover more than 100,000 pages of book, journal, and reference content to support your learning

find out more at
www.srmo.sagepub.com